NEWT

A COOKBOOK FOR ALL

NEWT NGUYEN

PHOTOGRAPHS BY
ANDREA D'AGOSTO

H
HARVEST
An Imprint of WILLIAM MORROW

TO MOM,

I'm sorry. I'll never be able to be the doctor that you'll
be able to brag about to your friends. However, at least
you can tell them that your son came out with this cool
cookbook. Thank you for being my first introduction to
cooking. When I first started making cooking videos, you
were confused but still showed your support by helping
me with the dishes while I edited on my laptop. Those
memories back in the mobile home will stay with me
forever. Hopefully by the time this book is released, you've
already beaten cancer and I've bought you the house
you've always wanted.

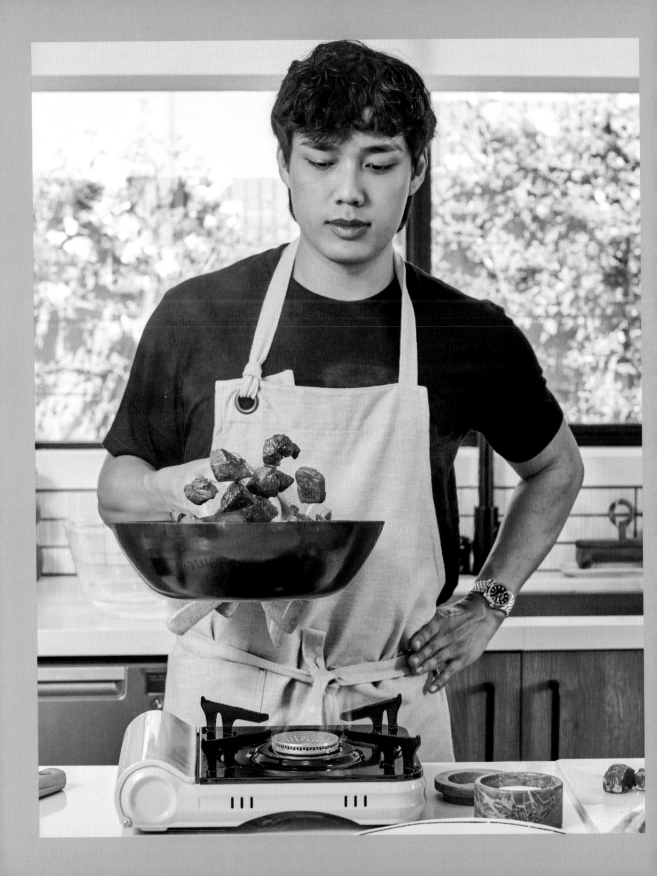

CONTENTS

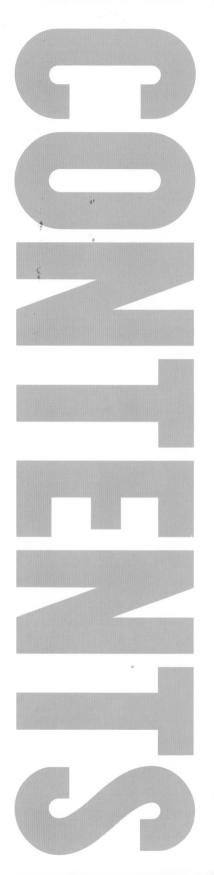

ACKNOWL

I truly believe that a person is only as great as the support system that surrounds them. I know we all want to believe that we're the main character in an anime and can solve all of life's problems, but girl . . . be so serious right now.

First, I want to thank my parents. Mom, thank you for being such a great cook. Watching you work your magic in the kitchen inspired me without me even knowing it. Because of your expertise, I'm now able to share some of our culture and family recipes with the world. To me, that's fucking amazing, because I feel like Vietnamese food is so criminally underrated—especially your chicken salad. Dad, thank you for just going along with the vibes at all times. I know for damn sure I did not get any cooking skills from you, since the only thing you know how to make is braised Spam in a sambal sauce.

I also want to thank my sister, Yvonne. If it wasn't for you working three jobs and eating at every fast food restaurant close to your workplaces, I probably wouldn't have started cooking. Thank you for allowing me to meal-prep for you even though I had zero cooking experience at first. Thank you for living with me temporarily while I was making this cookbook, too. Having such an experienced, professional eater was such a huge help to perfect all the seasonings for the recipes.

EDGMENTS

Thank you, Aria. You're the first friend I made when I moved to Los Angeles, and just also happen to be a great cook and an even *better* baker. When it comes to recipe testing, you provided insight here and there, and taught me cool pastry techniques along the way. I never had great baking skills, because my mom kept all of our baking sheets in the oven, but you inspire me to practice more.

Thank you to the team at Harvest and HarperCollins for believing in me and working with me on this cookbook. Shout-outs to Sarah Kwak and Eve Attermann for spearheading this entire cookbook and making sure I hit all of my deadlines (which I probably missed, but still, thank you). Thank you to my amazing recipe writer, Martha Rose Shulman, for transforming my third-grade writing skills into something that is way more comprehensible and that readers can actually understand and follow. Thank you to my amazing recipe testers, Karlee Rotoly and Danielle DeLott, for testing the recipes literally one month before they were due. Without you ladies, this entire cookbook would've been an absolute disaster. You guys are real ones fr.

Thank you to my entire photography team, Andrea D'Agosto, Ashli Buts, Nathan Carrabba, Courtney Weis, and Jaclyn Kershek. We spent about nine days straight in the studio cooking up photos for this cookbook. In that time, I definitely learned a lot about what it takes to produce great food photography, and I'll be applying it to my own content in the future. You guys are absolutely GOATED.

Shout-outs to Netflix even though you guys raised your prices recently and stopped spending on food shows. I still love you. Shout-out to *The Chef Show* with Jon Favreau and Roy Choi. During my depression era, I binge-watched so many episodes. That show was one of the main reasons I even wanted to start cooking in the first place. Jon Favreau and Roy Choi made cooking look *so* fun, and their personalities and chemistry were so entertaining that I felt like I had to get up to cook something. Since I moved to L.A., I actually ran into Roy Choi outside Sun Nong Dan on Western. It was the only time that I legitimately got starstruck. I froze up and couldn't muster up the courage to say hi or ask for a picture. Hopefully you guys read this and feel peer-pressured into cooking with me one day. That would be awesome.

A special shout-out goes to the Parsley gang, my supporters. Shout-outs to the Twitter and TikTok communities during the quarantine arc. Shit was really crazy back then and I hope I was able to entertain you guys with my cooking videos. More recently, shout-outs to my Instagram Reels and Facebook communities. I never thought I would be using Facebook again, but here we are. The cooking communities on Meta platforms have been so amazing.

Without all of your continuous and loving support, I would be nothing. You guys are my support system and have gotten me through really tough times. You gave me purpose when I had none. I'll never forget that, and I'll always try my absolute hardest to make you guys proud. Thank you.

Is cooking hard, or are you just being lazy?

NAHHHH, I'm just playing. I saw an opportunity to start the book off with a little gaslighting, and had to do it. In all seriousness though, everybody is capable of cooking. It's as easy as building IKEA furniture. First, gather all the parts, screws, and Allen keys. Then, open up the instruction manual and boot up your English 2 reading skills. Do what the instructions tell you to do, and you'll end up with a nice and sturdy piece of Scandinavian furniture. Cooking is essentially the same thing, except the end result of your work isn't limited to only one culture.

I wasn't always passionate about cooking. Seeing my persona online and how much I dedicate myself to cooking content, you would think I've been doing this for a long time. Perhaps my parents bought me an Easy-Bake Oven as a kid, I fell in love with it, and the rest was history? Maybe I was on *MasterChef Junior* and had dreams of becoming the best chef in the world ever since I was a kid? Absolutely not.

Don't get me wrong, I was always around food—but had more interest in eating it than making it. My mom is a talented Vietnamese cook who worked at numerous Vietnamese restaurants ever since she came to America in the 90s. My early encounters with great food were all the times I came home from

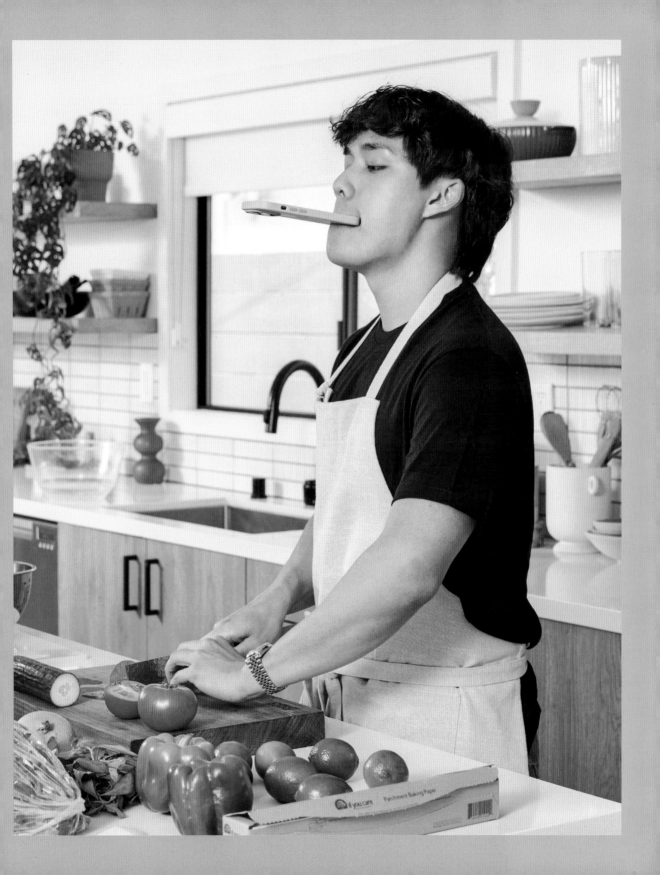

school, excited as I walked up my mobile home stairs because I could smell the delicious dinners that my mom was preparing for our family. You know the smell that I'm talking about. Onions and garlic sautéed in a pan? Ughh . . . bottle it, turn it into a perfume, and spray it all over me. (Pause.)

I got my first taste of cooking when I started to sell Spam musubis in high school. Spam musubis are these Hawaiian snacks of sushi rice packed into a rectangle, topped with furikake and Spam, then fried and caramelized in a sweet teriyaki/barbecue sauce. At least, this was how I made my Spam musubi, which is far from authentic, but authentically mine. Back then, I wanted to keep up with my friends who had new shoes, cool cars, etc., and there was no way in hell I was going to ask my parents, who were already trying their best to support my sister and me, for money. So, what did I do? Every night, my mom and I spent three to four hours making and wrapping eighty Spam musubis. The next morning, we would warm them up and give them to two employees (my friends) to sell in between classes and at lunch. My mom and I did that together, every school day for three years.

After high school, I worked even closer to food. My first job? Making pretzels at Auntie Anne's in a theme park. To this day, I remember it as one of my favorite jobs because I would secretly eat all the pretzels that we were required to throw away at the end of the night. I only worked there three months though, until I got a job working as a busboy/server/bartender/janitor at a Vietnamese restaurant/bar. It was at this restaurant that I was truly able to see how food went from ingredients being delivered to dishes enjoyed by restaurant goers. Many nights were spent watching the amazing kitchen staff prepare the meals for our customers. I loved watching them do their thing. The propane fires that lit up the woks, the head chef calling the shots and directing the line cooks, the insane chaos and stress that comes with working in this type of environment—I loved it all. But it still wasn't enough for me to get cooking.

Life works in mysterious ways. Sometimes it can feel like the world is against you, and then the next moment, all the stars line up to lead you to your destiny. I fell into depression at 20 years old. Balancing being a full-time college student, working closing shifts at a restaurant, and battling severe acne, eczema, and alopecia that almost took both of my eyebrows, I'd had enough. I quit my job. If I wasn't at school, I would be at home on my bed watching cooking shows on

Netflix and Twitch streams. This was my life for a year straight. I had no purpose and motivation, and gave up on myself.

By my 21st birthday, I was tired of feeling sorry for myself and wanted change. At this point, my sister was gaining weight rapidly because she worked three jobs and ate only fast food to save time. She needed someone to prepare meals for her. Having watched about a dozen cooking shows on Netflix and YouTube, I felt ready to challenge myself. I cooked a new recipe every day, for thirty days straight, so that my sister would have healthier meals, packed in to-go containers, ready for her to take to work. I did it. I felt accomplished seeing that cooking for my sister helped her change her life and live more healthily.

I didn't start making cooking videos right away though. I transferred schools and pursued a business degree. I still spent my free time watching more and more cooking videos and shows. I learned everything from different ways to cut vegetables to making stews, and about ingredients from all around the world. It wasn't until Popeyes came out with their Spicy Chicken Sandwich that I decided to get in front of a camera. If you remember the craze, you know that people were lining up around the block for the sandwich. And in my city, people were selling them out of their cars in parking lots. Disgusted by people's lack of access to fried chicken sandwiches, I took matters into my own hands. I filmed and posted a cooking tutorial on how to make a spicy chicken sandwich at home, and the rest is history.

"Okay, you just gave us your whole life story. That's great. But what the hell does that have to do with this book?"

CHILLLLL!!!! I'm getting there. Let me cook. The reason I wanted to come out with a cookbook is because, since I began posting videos, people would comment, "I wish I could cook as well as you." You can. I truly believe that anyone is capable of anything they put their mind to. I'm not anyone special. I wasn't born with insane cooking skills. I didn't attend a fancy cooking school like Le Cordon Bleu. I wasn't ever on a cooking competition show. I was just once a depressed kid, in his room, binge-watching cooking shows underneath his bedsheets. If I can learn how to cook, so can you.

I also wanted to make a book that was dedicated to kids who are in the same situation as I am—children of immigrants, and first- and second-generation Americans. Having immigrant parents means that you grew up eating your culture's food every day. For me, Vietnamese dishes like Caramelized Fish (Cá Kho Tộ, page 157), Phở (page 143), and Chicken Congee (Cháo Gà, page 22) were dinner staples that I ate for the majority of my life. But, I wasn't only limited to what my parents knew how to cook. Growing up in California, which is a melting pot of all cultures, I picked up some favorite foods, like Korean Short Ribs (Galbi, page 117), Thai Basil Chicken (Pad Krapow Gai, page 88), and Carne Asada Tostadas (page 69), along the way. For this book, I sat down with myself and had a "that's so Raven" moment. If I was going to write a book, I would need each recipe to have a purpose and a story. What foods made an impact on me as a kid? What stories can I tell? What would I want to see in a recipe book?

To me, this book is a "coming of age" cookbook. At the core, I'm Vietnamese, so we have to include my mom's recipes for the Vietnamese food that she's been making since I was a little kid and that now serve as the antidote for whenever I'm feeling homesick. I'm also American, so we tap into foods that are popular in the States, like smash burgers, vodka pasta, and chicken Parmesan. (I know the latter two are Italian.) As a San Jose native, I wanted to pay homage to my city with Mexican eats like elote, birria tacos, and the famous orange sauce (salsa roja) from La Vic's. Then we move on to the first city that I moved to, Los Angeles, where I'm constantly being spoiled by some of the best Korean, Thai, and Japanese food. This book highlights my food journey throughout my life, taking inspiration from the many cultures that I've been exposed to. If you can put me into a book, I think this would be it.

So, instead of relying on cup ramen to survive, take my hand. Let's walk through these recipes together and learn how to cook for ourselves. We got this.

When you go to a concert, the main act never performs first. Absolutely not. Otherwise, all the people that arrive fashionably late would miss everything and arrive just to clean up the trash left behind. Every show needs an opener. Someone that's capable of easing the audience and getting them into the right mood so that when the main performance arrives, everyone is hyped and ready to party the night away. For a proper meal, that opener would be the starters, sides, and soups.

Here, you'll find appetizers that I personally love to make and order at restaurants. For me, plain bread with butter as a starter is too boring. What's not boring, however, is garlic confit bread, wonton soup, and great hummus. All of these recipes can stand on their own, but some, like Garlic Mashed Potatoes and French Fries, are great paired with a main act, like Red Wine Braised Short Ribs or Smash Burgers.

1

OPENING ACTS

HUMMUS

MAKES ABOUT 2 SERVINGS

I'm not a bean person. Whenever I eat beans, I get gassy to the point where it's detrimental to my health and those around me. No amount of air freshener can save the room. However, I *love* hummus. Do you see the problem here?

Hummus is one of those dips that I discovered in my twenties, and I wish someone had told me about it sooner. It's high in fiber, is a great source of protein, and has healthy fat. Basically, you should be eating hummus because it's good for you. Not only is this recipe very easy to make, but it yields some of the smoothest hummus I've ever had.

FYI, chickpeas and garbanzo beans are the same thing. I just wanted to make that clear because the first time I made hummus, I spent 30 minutes at Whole Foods, stressed out, because I couldn't find the chickpeas. I even asked a worker to help me out and he was just as lost as I was.

One 15-ounce can chickpeas (aka garbanzo beans)

½ teaspoon baking soda

½ cup tahini

5 tablespoons lemon juice

2 tablespoons cold water, plus more as needed

8 cloves Garlic Confit (page 191)

1 teaspoon ground cumin

1 teaspoon kosher salt

Paprika, for dusting

Chopped fresh parsley

1. Drain the chickpeas in a strainer, rinse, and transfer to a medium saucepan. Add enough water (about 3 cups) to cover the chickpeas by an inch. Add the baking soda and mix well. Bring to a boil over medium heat, then reduce to a simmer and cook over medium-low heat for 20 minutes. Drain and set aside.

2. In a food processor, combine the tahini, lemon juice, cold water, garlic confit, cumin, and salt. Blend until the mixture is fluffy and airy, 1 to 2 minutes. In two or three separate additions, add the chickpeas to the food processor and blend in 15-second increments. Depending on the consistency desired, keep blending, incorporating 1 tablespoon of cold water at a time, until the hummus reaches the desired smoothness. The more water you add, the smoother/runnier the hummus will be.

3. Transfer the hummus to a plate, dust with paprika, and sprinkle with chopped parsley. Serve with lavash or naan.

GOODBYE GRAINY HUMMUS!

Why simmer the chickpeas with baking soda? And why simmer canned chickpeas, if they're already cooked? Smooth hummus. Although canned chickpeas are already cooked, they're not nearly soft enough to make a smooth hummus. If you use them straight from the can, you'll get a hummus with a grainy texture. You might've heard people swearing by soaking chickpeas overnight, or spending copious amounts of time and effort peeling the skin off of each individual bean. Although that method works, this is a much more efficient way to address the skins. When cooked together, baking soda helps break down the skin of the chickpeas, and allows for the beans to cook faster. The resulting beans and their skins are very soft and blend out smoothly. Goodbye, grainy hummus! You won't be missed.

GUACAMOLE

SERVES 2, AS AN APPETIZER

Every time I order guacamole at a restaurant, I have to turn down the brightness on my phone and check my bank account first to see if I have the funds. Why on earth is it so expensive in L.A.? Being in California, avocados are affordable. The average cost for one is about a dollar. So it's insane to me how restaurants charge an arm and a leg for some guac.

There's a restaurant on Melrose (I won't name names) that charged me twenty dollars for some chips and guac. Stuck between buying it to use the restroom or peeing my pants, I had no other options. This recipe is 100 percent out of pettiness. I know the authentic taquerias wouldn't do me like this. *sniffles*

3 ripe medium avocados

1 teaspoon kosher salt

½ white onion, minced

1 Roma tomato, cored, seeded, and minced

½ jalapeño chile, cored, seeded, and minced

Juice of ½ lime

¼ cup minced fresh cilantro

1. Cut the avocados in half, throw away the pits, and scoop the flesh into a medium mixing bowl. Add the salt and mash the avocados with a fork to desired consistency (I prefer it a bit chunky).

2. Stir in the onion, tomato, jalapeño, lime juice, and cilantro. Mix well and adjust for salt as needed. Serve with a side of chips, or in tacos, or inside burritos, etc., etc. Enjoy!

MAC SALAD

SERVES 6, AS A SIDE

Mac salad, yummy yummy. You can't complete a Hawaiian meal without eating mac salad—it's against the rules. For those who are uncultured, having macaroni in a salad might be odd at first. The fact that it's served cold may come off even more odd. But once your taste buds are matured and high-leveled like mine, you're going to wonder how you lived without it. Creamy, tangy, and slightly sweet, it's my favorite salad to pair with Chicken Katsu (page 51) or Korean Short Ribs (page 117).

2 teaspoons kosher salt

4 ounces elbow macaroni

1 tablespoon red wine vinegar

2 tablespoons shredded carrot

2 tablespoons minced celery

2 tablespoons grated yellow onion

¾ cup mayonnaise

2½ tablespoons whole milk

2 tablespoons sugar

2 teaspoons garlic powder

½ teaspoon freshly ground black pepper

¼ teaspoon MSG

1. Fill a medium pot halfway with water, add 1½ teaspoons of the salt, and bring to a boil over high heat. Add the macaroni and cook for 5 minutes past the recommended time on the box (about 14 minutes). The texture of the pasta should be soft and easy to eat but not mushy.

2. Drain the pasta and transfer to a large mixing bowl. Add the vinegar and mix well. Cover and cool in the fridge for 15 minutes.

3. Add all the remaining ingredients plus the remaining ½ teaspoon salt to the pasta and mix together thoroughly with your hands. Since there's a lot of different seasonings, it's important to make sure each noodle gets some love. Cover with plastic wrap and refrigerate for at least 2 hours, or up to 3 days, to allow the noodles to soak up the flavors.

4. When ready to eat, serve as a side. Enjoy!

FREE GAME

If you don't have a potato ricer, you can push the potatoes through a strainer and stir with a rubber spatula to get a nice, smooth mash. You could also use a potato masher, but for the really smooth puree, you want to then push the potatoes through a strainer.

GARLIC MASHED POTATOES

SERVES 2 TO 3, AS A SIDE

Potatoes—the most yummy and versatile vegetable out there. But mash potatoes? *Ouuuwwwee!* The first time I made this recipe and brought it to a potluck, all my friends loved it and kept asking for the recipe—but I said wait for the cookbook to come out.

What sets this apart from regular mashed potatoes is the use of garlic, half-and-half, and butter—lots of it. When you're making mashed potatoes, it's important to throw calories out the window, because this is not healthy at all. But that's okay, the diet starts on Monday.

2 medium russet potatoes (about 1 pound), peeled and cut into 1-inch pieces (see Note)

1 tablespoon kosher salt, for the cooking water

⅓ cup half-and-half

½ cup (1 stick) salted butter

¾ teaspoon garlic salt, or 2 heads Garlic Confit (page 191) plus ½ teaspoon kosher salt

¼ teaspoon freshly ground black pepper

Butter pats or gravy, for serving (optional)

Chopped fresh parsley or chives, for garnish (optional)

NOTE: *The potato pieces should all be the same size so they cook evenly.*

1. In a medium saucepan or pot, combine the potatoes, salt, and enough cold water to cover the potatoes (about 4 cups). Place over medium heat, bring to a gentle boil, and boil gently until fork tender, 16 to 18 minutes.

2. While the potatoes are cooking, combine the half-and-half and butter in a small saucepan and heat over medium-low heat until the butter melts and the mixture is uniformly warm. Do not allow the mixture to simmer or boil. Keep warm.

3. When the potatoes are fork tender, drain and return to the pot. Allow the potatoes to steam uncovered in the pot until the excess moisture has evaporated and the potatoes are dry, usually 1 to 2 minutes. (Allowing the potatoes to steam and dry out after draining prevents watery mashed potatoes.)

4. Pass the potatoes through a potato ricer into a mixing bowl. Slowly incorporate the buttery half-and-half mixture, mixing well with a spatula or spoon. Add the garlic salt and pepper and combine well. (If using garlic confit and salt instead of garlic salt, add them to the mixing bowl before the potatoes. Using a fork, mash the confit, using the salt as an abrasive to help turn it into a paste. Then, pass the potatoes through a potato ricer into the bowl, mix, and season with pepper. See Free Game, opposite.)

5. Serve at once, hot, topped with butter pats or gravy, and parsley or chives, if desired.

CHEESY GARLIC BREAD

SERVES 4 TO 5, AS A SIDE

Why am I drooling? Maybe it's because we're making the most delicioso cheesy garlic bread ever. The first garlic bread I ever had was from the frozen section at Walmart—Texas garlic toast. I snuck it into my mom's shopping cart when she wasn't looking. Did I finish the whole box before my sister could get to it? Maybe. But was it yummy? Yes. Here is my version of the garlic toast that I loved as a kid (and still do). I like to pair it with Chicken Parm (page 114) or Pasta Pomodoro with Meatballs (page 106), but most of the time I just eat it by itself.

1 French baguette (about 20 inches long)

½ cup (1 stick) salted butter, softened

Cloves from 3 heads Garlic Confit (page 191)

¼ cup grated Parmesan

1 teaspoon red pepper flakes

1 teaspoon Italian seasoning

⅔ cup shredded mozzarella cheese

FOR TOPPING

Finely minced fresh parsley, to taste

Red pepper flakes, to taste

Maldon sea salt flakes, to taste

1. Preheat the oven to 350°F. Cut the baguette in half horizontally and transfer to a baking sheet. If it is too long, cut each half in half crosswise.

2. In a small bowl, mix the softened butter, garlic confit, Parmesan, red pepper flakes, and Italian seasoning. Using a small spatula or spoon, spread a layer of the butter mixture over each baguette half. Sprinkle the mozzarella on top.

3. Bake until the bread is nice and crispy on the outside and the cheese on top has melted, 18 to 20 minutes. Top with toppings of choice and enjoy!

FRENCH FRIES

SERVES 2, AS A SIDE

French fries are one of those things that I really never cared about learning how to make.

Why would I ever cook fries from scratch when McDonald's is literally across the street? Besides that, you can get prepackaged french fries in the freezer section of any grocery store. Work smarter, not harder. Duh. I couldn't have been more wrong.

French fries from scratch are absolutely unbeatable. This is my personal favorite recipe, as we parboil the potatoes before double-frying and seasoning with salt and fresh thyme. The result is an unbelievably crispy exterior and a soft pillowy inside. You're still probably going to go to a fast food restaurant to satisfy your cravings though. But if you find yourself being extra or having time, you can't go wrong with making them at home.

2 large russet potatoes, about 1½ pounds

1 tablespoon kosher salt, plus more to taste

Vegetable or canola oil, for frying

1½ tablespoons minced fresh thyme

1. Peel the potatoes and cut into ½-inch-thick sticks. If your potatoes are too long (over 6 inches), cut the fries in half. Place in a large pot and run under cold water, rubbing them to clean them of excess starch. Drain and cover with enough cold water to completely submerge.

2. Add the salt to the pot and mix. Bring to a boil over medium-high heat, then lower the heat to maintain a simmer. Simmer the potatoes until tender, about 10 minutes. Drain the potatoes and transfer to a paper towel–lined baking sheet to cool.

3. Rinse and dry the pan, and return to the stove. Add 2 inches of oil and heat to 325°F over medium-high heat.

4. Once the oil is ready, fry half of the potatoes for 6 minutes, until lightly golden. Remove from the oil with a strainer or skimmer, and set aside. Repeat with the other half of the potatoes.

5. Turn up the heat and allow the oil to reach 375°F. Add half the potatoes and fry again until crispy and golden, about 2 minutes. Transfer to a bowl and season with fresh thyme and salt to taste. Repeat with the other half of the potatoes. Mix well and serve hot. Enjoy!

BANG-BANG SHRIMP

SERVES 3 TO 4, AS AN APPETIZER

Bang-bang shrimp is my ideal type of appetizer. It has all the flavors I like: spicy, sweet, creamy. It's also crunchy and fun to eat. It's *also* my first ever recipe that made it into a cookbook, the official TikTok one: *As Cooked on TikTok*. However, you know I had to withhold some secrets and give them a great value version instead. This version uses eggs as a binder for the panko breading instead of buttermilk. I prefer egg because the batter sticks on better. Also, for the sauce, we use a bit of honey to sweeten and thicken things up.

Serve on a bed of lettuce as an appetizer or use smaller shrimp and serve as shrimp tacos. The world is your oyster, I'm just living in it.

FOR THE SHRIMP

1 pound large shrimp, peeled and deveined

1 teaspoon garlic salt

1 teaspoon onion powder

½ teaspoon smoked paprika

3 tablespoons cornstarch

2 large egg whites

1 large egg yolk

2 tablespoons milk

1½ cups panko breadcrumbs

Vegetable or canola oil, for frying

FOR THE BANG-BANG SAUCE

2 tablespoons mayonnaise

1 tablespoon sweet chili sauce

1 tablespoon sriracha

½ teaspoon honey

1 tablespoon sliced fresh chives

1. Place the shrimp in a large mixing bowl and add the garlic salt, onion powder, and paprika. Mix well, then add the cornstarch. Mix until the shrimp are evenly coated with cornstarch and set aside.

2. Prepare two shallow bowls: Beat the egg whites, egg yolk, and milk in one bowl (I crack 2 eggs into the bowl and take one of the yolks out). Place the panko in the second bowl.

3. Coat one shrimp with the egg mixture and transfer to the breadcrumbs. Using your fingers, press the breadcrumbs onto the shrimp, so that the breading doesn't fall off during the frying process. Transfer to a plate. Repeat until all the shrimp are breaded.

4. In a medium pot, heat 2 inches of oil to 350°F over medium heat. In batches, fry the shrimp until golden brown, about 2 minutes. Transfer to a paper towel–lined plate.

5. For the sauce, mix the mayonnaise, chili sauce, sriracha, and honey in a small bowl. Transfer the shrimp to a serving plate, then drizzle with the sauce. Top with chives and serve.

SHRIMP TOAST

MAKES 10 PIECES

Nothing can unlock a childhood memory like food can, and this shrimp toast does it for me every time. Growing up, it didn't matter what the occasion was. Whether a birthday, anniversary, or funeral, this toast was always present with perfect attendance. When you make a plate to eat at one of these gatherings, it would typically look like: fried rice, some grilled chicken, maybe a few egg rolls. For me? My plate was filled with only shrimp toast. That creamy, cheesy shrimp blend that sat on top of a slightly crispy baguette? That's something I could never get enough of.

8 ounces shrimp, peeled and deveined

¾ cup grated Mexican cheese blend

¼ cup Kewpie mayo

2 scallions, sliced

2 teaspoons garlic powder

1 teaspoon onion powder

1 teaspoon chicken bouillon powder

1 teaspoon sugar

¼ teaspoon freshly ground black pepper

1 French baguette, cut diagonally into ¾-inch-thick slices (10 pieces)

Minced fresh parsley, for garnish

1. Preheat the oven to 350°F and position one rack in the middle and one near the top. Line a baking sheet with foil.

2. Mince the shrimp very finely, to a paste-like consistency, and place in a mixing bowl. Add the cheese, mayo, scallions, garlic powder, onion powder, bouillon powder, sugar, and pepper. Using your hands, mix the ingredients together until thoroughly combined.

3. Using a small spatula or spoon, spread a generous layer (a couple of generous tablespoons) of the shrimp mixture over the top surface of each bread piece, and place on the lined baking sheet.

4. Bake on the middle rack until the shrimp is cooked through and the bread is crispy on the outsides, about 25 minutes. Switch the oven to broil, move the baking sheet to the higher rack, and broil until the cheese is nicely browned, an additional 1 to 2 minutes. Garnish with parsley and serve!

MISO SOUP

SERVES 4

Growing up means you have to start worrying about probiotics. Ew, I hate what I just said. Am I becoming a boomer?

The reason I bring up probiotics is because miso soup has a lot of them. I mean, what's not to like about miso soup? It's healthy for your gut, easy to make, and tastes absolutely delicious.

Whenever I'm eating in a Japanese restaurant, I always order a small bowl to sip on. It makes me feel like I'm being proactive and taking care of my well-being. It also scientifically cancels out all the fried foods I've eaten that week. It's crazy how that works.

Miso soup is made from dashi, which is an essential stock in Japanese cuisine. The dashi that we make is a very basic one, containing kombu (dried kelp), bonito flakes (dried tuna), and water. Take this dashi and add in some wakame, soft tofu, and miso paste? Bow-chicka-wow-wow. We have a savory, umami, and light soup to complement any meal.

About ½ ounce kombu (about a 7x8-inch piece)

4 cups water

About ½ ounce bonito flakes (1½ cups)

4 ounces soft tofu, cut into ½-inch cubes

2 tablespoons wakame

2 tablespoons white miso

1 scallion (green part only), sliced

1. First make the dashi (Japanese stock). In a medium pot, combine the kombu and water and bring to just under a boil over medium-low heat; this should take 10 to 12 minutes. It's important not to let the kombu boil, because it will become a bit slimy, and this changes the consistency of the broth.

2. Using tongs, remove and discard the kombu. Add the bonito flakes, leave on the heat for 30 seconds, then remove from the heat. Strain the dashi through a fine-mesh sieve into a bowl.

3. Return the broth to the pot, place over medium heat, and bring to a boil. Once the dashi is boiling, add the diced soft tofu and wakame. Cook for 3 to 4 minutes, then remove from heat.

4. Stir in the white miso by pushing it through a sieve into the dashi broth. This removes any lumps and ensures that the miso will be nice and smooth.

5. Serve at once, topping each bowl with sliced scallion.

NOTE: *Wakame is the "crunchy" seaweed that is often served with miso soup. It's sold in a dried form and can be found in most Asian supermarkets.*

TOMATO SOUP

SERVES 3

As someone who grew up hating tomatoes, the fact that this recipe is in my book blows my mind. That's like a cookbook author hating pickles and creating pickle soup (which I also hate and sounds absolutely *vile,* btw). I think this is my way of declaring peace between myself and all the tomato lovers out there.

Tomato soup was one of those food discoveries that I made as I was scrolling on TikTok one fall season. I had no idea the cultural impact it had in American culture, but it seemed like something I could get on board with. We start by oven roasting tomatoes, onions, and garlic until slightly charred. Then into the blender it all goes with a hearty chicken broth and cream. The result is an absolute flavor bomb, but my favorite thing about it is the "homey-ness." When I eat this with a Grilled Cheese (page 54), it feels like being wrapped up in a blanket in bed on a cold winter day.

2 pounds Roma tomatoes, halved lengthwise, cored, and seeded

1 yellow onion, cut into 1-inch pieces

8 garlic cloves, peeled

¼ cup plus 1 tablespoon olive oil, plus more to taste

2 teaspoons kosher salt

½ teaspoon freshly ground black pepper, plus more to taste

¼ cup tomato paste

1½ cups chicken broth

½ cup heavy cream, plus more to taste

1 tablespoon sugar

1 teaspoon dried oregano

1 teaspoon celery salt

Fresh basil leaves, for garnish

1. Preheat the oven to 425°F and position a rack in the middle.

2. Place the tomatoes, cut side up, on a large baking sheet, along with the onion and garlic cloves. Drizzle on the ¼ cup olive oil and sprinkle with the salt and pepper. Bake until the vegetables are slightly blistered, 40 to 45 minutes.

3. About 10 minutes before the tomatoes are done, heat the remaining 1 tablespoon oil in a medium saucepan over medium heat. Add the tomato paste and cook, stirring, until caramelized, about 4 minutes. Stir in the broth and cream and bring to a simmer. Transfer to a blender.

4. Transfer the tomatoes, onions, garlic, and all the juices from the baking sheet to the blender. Add the sugar, oregano, and celery salt and blend on medium-low until smooth, about 1 minute.

5. Taste and adjust for salt, if needed. Transfer to serving bowls and top with additional olive oil, cream, pepper, and a few basil leaves. Serve, with grilled cheese sandwiches, if desired!

WONTON SOUP

SERVES 4, MAKES 36 TO 40 WONTONS

Wonton soup is my favorite soup when I'm feeling like a skinny legend. No noodles, no vegetables—just give me a bunch of wontons in a seasoned chicken broth. I mean, how can something be so perfect? Wontons are like little presents of deliciousness filled with pork and shrimp, waiting to be unwrapped and devoured. I never got presents as a kid, so maybe this is my way of healing my inner child. My favorite thing about it is that the wontons can be made ahead of time. Just wrap a bunch and throw them into the freezer for whenever you're hungry (see Free Game). And whenever I'm in a time pinch, I'm a fan of buying frozen Chinese wontons from 99 Ranch Market and using them instead.

FOR THE WONTONS

8 ounces ground pork

4 ounces peeled and deveined shrimp, finely minced

1 scallion, minced

3 garlic cloves, finely minced

1 teaspoon grated fresh ginger

1½ tablespoons soy sauce

1 teaspoon sesame oil

½ teaspoon sugar

¼ teaspoon baking soda

¼ teaspoon kosher salt

¼ teaspoon white pepper

40 wonton wrappers, preferably yellow wrappers

1. Combine the filling ingredients for the wontons (everything except the wrappers) in a large mixing bowl and mix well with your hands. Shape your hand into a claw shape to facilitate mixing. This way the ingredients will be well combined but the filling won't be dense and tough.

2. To make the wontons, place a wrapper in your hand. Using a small spoon, scoop about 1½ teaspoons filling into the middle of the wrapper. Dip your finger in a small bowl of water and outline the border of the wrapper. Pinch together the top and bottom corners of the wrapper, and then scrunch both of the sides to create a "comet"-shaped wonton. Place the wonton on a baking sheet and cover with a kitchen towel. (Wrapping all of the wontons will take a while, so be sure to cover the wontons with a kitchen towel as you fill them to prevent them from drying out. Also, using yellow wonton skins will make the end product more visually appealing compared to white skins.) Once all of the wontons are made, cover with plastic wrap and freeze overnight.

3. For the soup, when ready to eat, combine all of the soup ingredients in a medium pot. Bring to a simmer over medium-high heat, turn off the heat, and set aside while you cook the bok choy and wontons.

recipe continues

FOR THE SOUP

2 quarts chicken broth

4 small fresh ginger slices

6 garlic cloves, peeled and slightly smashed

4 scallions, white parts only, ends trimmed, left whole

2 teaspoons fish sauce

2 teaspoons light soy sauce

FOR TOPPING

2 bunches baby bok choy, halved lengthwise

Green parts of 2 scallions, sliced

Chili oil, to taste (optional)

4. In a separate pot, bring 3 inches of salted water to a boil. Quickly blanch the bok choy until it turns vibrant green and tender, 30 to 45 seconds, then remove with tongs and set aside.

5. Bring the water back to a rolling boil and add a quarter of the wontons. Give the wontons a stir to prevent them from sticking to the bottom of the pot. Cook for 4 to 5 minutes, until they are cooked all the way through and floating to the top.

6. Using a skimmer or a slotted spoon, remove the wontons from the water and divide between two bowls. Repeat with the remaining wontons and divide them between another two bowls.

7. Remove the garlic, ginger, and white part of scallions from the soup, and bring it to a simmer once again. Ladle the soup evenly into the bowls. Top with the baby bok choy halves, the sliced scallion greens, and chili oil if desired.

FREE GAME

If you want to prepare the wontons ahead of time, you can store them a ziplock bag in the freezer until ready to use, for up to 2 months. Don't thaw; cook directly from the freezer following the directions in Step 5.

CHICKEN CONGEE (CHÁO GÀ)

SERVES 2

I've had congee since I was a little baby. It's our version of oatmeal, but instead of oats, it's made with rice. There are many different variations of congee and it has many different names around the world. But in my household, the most popular version is cháo gà, or Vietnamese chicken congee. The flavors are subtle, made of chicken broth, shredded chicken, ginger, salt, pepper, and a dash of fish sauce for the culture. It feels like a warm hug, especially on days you're not feeling well.

½ cup short-grain rice

6 cups water

3 slices fresh ginger

1½ teaspoons Vietnamese chicken bouillon (preferably Totole brand)

½ teaspoon kosher salt

2 bone-in skin-on chicken thighs

1½ teaspoons fish sauce

FOR TOPPING

Freshly ground black pepper, to taste

1 knob fresh ginger, finely julienned

Scallions, sliced

Chopped fresh cilantro, to taste

Chili oil (optional)

Fried Shallots (optional, page 194)

1. Place the rice in a medium pot and wash with warm water. Use your fingers to agitate the rice and release the starch. Drain all of the water and place the pot on the stove over medium heat.

2. Add the water to the rice, along with the ginger slices, chicken bouillon, and salt. Bring the mixture to a boil, then reduce the heat to low to maintain a simmer. Set a timer for 40 minutes and go on to the next step.

3. Add the chicken thighs to the pot, and cook until the chicken is cooked through with an internal temperature of 165°F, about 25 minutes, depending on the size of the thighs. When the chicken is thoroughly cooked, remove from the pot and set aside until cool enough to handle (about 15 minutes). Using your hands, shred the chicken into bite-size pieces and set aside.

4. When the timer rings, the porridge is just about done! Whisk vigorously to break apart the rice grains. Check the consistency to see if it's to your liking. If you want a runnier porridge, add water, about ¼ cup at a time, and stir until it reaches the desired consistency. Season with fish sauce and mix one last time before removing from heat.

5. Divide the porridge between two bowls and top with the shredded chicken, pepper, julienned ginger, scallions, and cilantro. Drizzle chili oil on top and sprinkle with fried shallots, if using. Enjoy!

I'm not gonna lie to you, I do not eat that many vegetables. I'm not *opposed* to eating them more often. It's not like I'm allergic or anything. However, I do find them really . . . boring? Why fill your stomach with a plant, when you can save your stomach to indulge in an entire plate of fried chicken wings or focus on the main course instead? The latter option sounds a lot better to me.

That said, I still wanted to include a vegetable chapter in my cookbook. Morally speaking, as a food influencer, I should *somewhat* encourage my viewers, or readers, to eat more nutritious foods. I, myself, need a reminder from time to time to eat more vegetables. It's the least I could do to cancel out all the fried foods that I consume on a weekly basis. Although it is a short list, these are the favorite vegetable recipes that I gravitate towards.

2

FINE, I'LL EAT MY VEGETABLES

ASIAN CUCUMBER SALAD

SERVES 2

What's green and red, but not Christmas? Asian cucumber salad. Ba-dum-tsssssss. It's actually one of the only salads that I'll ever eat. It's crunchy, refreshing, flavorful, and spicy. But more importantly it's simple, addictive, and super easy to make. A perfect side to eat with Korean BBQ or any grilled meats.

4 Persian or mini cucumbers

1 tablespoon kosher salt

2 tablespoons garlic chili oil (I like S&B brand)

2 tablespoons rice vinegar

2½ teaspoons sugar

2 teaspoons gochugaru (Korean pepper flakes)

½ teaspoon sesame oil

¼ teaspoon MSG

Toasted sesame seeds, for topping

1. Rinse the cucumbers and slice off the ends. Cut into ½-inch-thick slices and transfer to a bowl. Add the salt and mix well. (Salting the cucumbers helps extract the water from the inside, which makes them crunchier.) Refrigerate for 30 minutes.

2. In a small mixing bowl, combine the chili oil, vinegar, sugar, gochugaru, sesame oil, and MSG and mix well.

3. Rinse the cucumber slices with cold water. Drain well and transfer to a bowl.

4. Pour the sauce over the cucumbers and mix well. Transfer to a serving plate and top with toasted sesame seeds. Enjoy!

PARMESAN ASPARAGUS

SERVES 2

Do we need another vegetable recipe? Well, here's a-spar-agus ("a spare, I guess!"). Was that funny? No? My sister came up with that one, and if it wasn't, then she will be sleeping outside on the streets tonight.

Asparagus is a wonderful vegetable when cooked properly. This recipe is foolproof because all you have to do is roast the spears in the oven. We spice things up by adding panko breadcrumbs, which gives us a nice crunchy texture to pair with the tender veggie. My favorite thing is to serve this with loads of grated Parmesan.

1 pound asparagus

1½ tablespoons olive oil

1 teaspoon garlic powder

1 teaspoon onion powder

¼ teaspoon kosher salt

2 tablespoons panko breadcrumbs

Freshly grated Parmesan, for topping, to taste

Lime wedges, for serving

1. Preheat the oven to 400°F and position a rack in the middle. Line a baking sheet (9x13 inches or larger) with foil.

2. Wash the asparagus. Cut off and discard the bottom inch of each stalk. Dry the asparagus and transfer to the foil-lined baking sheet. Drizzle with the olive oil and season with the garlic powder, onion powder, and salt. Using your hands or a pair of tongs, toss the asparagus until evenly covered, then sprinkle with the panko. Roast until the asparagus is tender and the breadcrumbs are golden, 12 to 14 minutes, depending on the thickness of the asparagus.

3. Transfer to a serving plate. Top with grated Parmesan and serve with wedges of lime.

CHILI OIL BROCCOLINI

SERVES 2

Wow, I'm really surprising myself with all these vegetable dishes. Broccolini is one of those that I don't mind having. It's the cooler younger brother of broccoli, which makes sense because it's a lot taller. One of the best ways to cook this veggie is to char it. I don't know what it is, but the char flavor is . . . hold on, let me get my thesaurus . . . scrumptious! It's typically a lot easier to char food when cooking on a grill, due to the open fire. However, with this method, we're charring the broccolini by cooking it on high heat. I like having the broccolini as a sidekick to main proteins like fish, steak, or chicken.

8 ounces broccolini

1 teaspoon olive oil

2 tablespoons unsalted butter

4 garlic cloves, thinly sliced

¼ teaspoon kosher salt, or more to taste

¼ teaspoon freshly ground black pepper, or more to taste

2 teaspoons chili oil, for topping

Lemon wedges, for serving

1. Wash the broccolini and dry well. Pluck off any leaves. Chop 1 inch off the bottom of the stalks and discard. If any of the stalks are thick, cut in half lengthwise.

2. Combine the broccolini with ¼ cup water in a medium pan. Cover and steam over medium heat until bright green and slightly tender, 3 to 4 minutes. Uncover and let any remaining water evaporate, then drizzle on the olive oil. Raise the heat to medium-high and continue to cook, turning with tongs every minute or so, until the broccolini is evenly charred throughout, about 3 minutes. (Don't turn it too often, as it needs to properly char.)

3. Turn off the heat and add the butter and garlic to one side of the pan. Let the butter melt and toast the garlic, about 30 seconds. Toss the broccolini with the garlic and butter, then season with salt and pepper to taste. Mix one last time before transferring to a serving plate.

4. Serve with your chili oil of choice and wedges of lemon.

GARLIC GREEN BEANS

SERVES 2

Surprisingly, I do eat more than one kind of vegetable. Ladies and gentlemen, I present to you—garlic green beans. It's a universally loved dish amongst Asian people, and recently trended on TikTok due to a restaurant called Din Tai Fung. To be clear, they didn't invent that shit. It's available at almost every Chinese restaurant on this planet. Still, I'm glad more people are finding out about it and eating more vegetables. It doesn't require many ingredients at all, and comes together super quick. There's no way anyone can mess this up . . . unless?

1 cup vegetable or canola oil, for frying

12 ounces green beans, washed and trimmed

8 garlic cloves, minced

2 teaspoons sugar

1 teaspoon kosher salt

Pinch of MSG

Chili oil, for topping (to spice things up; optional)

1. Heat the oil in a wok over high heat to 350°F.

2. Add the green beans and fry until slightly wilted and cooked all the way through, about 3 minutes. Using a skimmer or tongs, remove the green beans from the oil and set aside. Transfer all but 1 tablespoon of the oil to a heatproof glass bowl or measuring cup, let cool, then discard.

3. Place the wok back on the heat and reduce the heat to medium-low. Make sure the oil is not too hot, then add the garlic and cook until golden and fragrant, about 30 seconds.

4. Return the green beans to the wok, along with the sugar, salt, and MSG. Give everything one last toss to make sure the ingredients are mixed together well. Remove from heat and transfer to a serving plate. Enjoy with a drizzle of chili oil if you like!

ELOTE

SERVES 3

1 tablespoon kosher salt

3 ears of corn

½ cup grated cotija cheese
(about 2 ounces)

3 tablespoons salted
butter, softened

3 tablespoons mayonnaise

2 teaspoons chili powder

1 tablespoon minced fresh
cilantro, for garnish

4 or 5 lime wedges, for
serving

Valentina hot sauce, for
serving (optional)

Special equipment: 3
wooden chopsticks or
skewers

I loved growing up in California. It's a melting pot of cultures, and where I come from Mexicans and Asians stuck together like glue. TWINZIESSS. Despite the language barrier, we share a lot of similarities: Parents escaping to America in search of a better life for their future kids, the struggles in balancing this new American culture and carrying on the culture of your own people, you know the deal.

The first Mexican person I knew was my local elote man. As early as I can remember, he would come by my neighborhood every day, pushing a cart full of fixings for made-to-order shaved ice drinks (Raspados), loaded chips (Chicharrones de Harina), and corn. Even from inside my mobile home, I was made aware of his presence because he would ring this little bell that hung from his cart. My favorite thing to get from him was the elote. From an ice cooler, he would grab a piece of steamed corn, stab it with a wooden chopstick, and get to work. I would stand there with my sister, in awe, watching him as he painted on butter and mayo, then sprinkled on cotija cheese. In unison, my sister and I would tell him, "More cheese! More cheese!" and he would laugh as he hooked us up with more. Any day that I was able to gather enough money to buy elote was the best day ever. These days, I'm fortunate enough to be able to re-create elote at home myself! It's super easy (the hardest part is boiling water), and every time I make it, I'm reminded of my younger days at home.

1. Bring a large pot of water to a boil over high heat, then add the salt.

2. Meanwhile, husk the corn and remove any remaining corn silk. (I personally chop off both ends of the corn, since that's the area where some kernels will be missing. This is just an aesthetic preference.) Place the grated cotija on a plate and set aside for later.

3. Add the corn to the boiling salted water and cook until bright yellow and cooked through, about 5 minutes.

4. Remove the corn from the water, and insert a wooden chopstick or skewer into the bottom end of each ear. Using a pastry brush, brush on the butter, followed by the mayonnaise.

5. Place the corn, tip down, on the plate of cotija cheese. Using a spoon, spoon the cheese onto the corn, while rotating it. Then, sprinkle evenly with the chili powder. Set aside on a serving plate and repeat with the two remaining ears.

6. Top with cilantro, and serve with a side of lime wedges. It's common to drizzle on hot sauce (typically Valentina), but I prefer it without.

Fried chicken is my first love. Period. Stamp it, put it in an envelope, and mail it away. Before I even signed a deal for my book, I knew I was going to include a fried chicken section, because it's an important part of who I am. If you ever see me go on a long break without eating it, just know it's a cry for help and I'm not being myself.

I eat some form of fried chicken multiple times a week. My highest streak was when I went to Korea and ate it for ten days straight. The fried chicken delivery there comes very fast (15 to 30 minutes max). The chicken itself is double fried, which makes it very crispy and satisfying to bite into, and the meat is always packed with flavor. Fried chicken in Korea is actually *different*!

Not every story has a happy ending, though, because recently I discovered I have high cholesterol. To lower my cholesterol, I have to lose weight and eat less fried food. I went from eating my favorite food five times a week to only two times. But every now and then, I relapse and go on a bender once more.

To a beginner, frying chicken might seem daunting, but I promise you it isn't. Frying chicken is actually very easy and foolproof, especially if you're using a food/frying thermometer!

These are some of my favorite fried chicken variations. Telling me to pick one favorite chicken recipe is like asking me, in a life-or-death scenario, would I rather save my mom or dad. I plead the fifth. However, if you were to ask me which recipe is the most iconic to *me,* I'd say the Butter Wings (page 38). You can learn more about them when you get to read up on its page, but for now, I hope all my fried chicken lovers out there feel represented. I love us <3.

FRIED CHIMKEN

BUTTER WINGS

SERVES 3 TO 4

I worked at a Vietnamese restaurant for two years before I became an influencer. Yes, that's right. I want to set the record straight, because I feel like people have the misconception that influencers aren't hardworking. I'm different from the rest. Pick me! Choose me!

During this era in my life, I went to school from 7 A.M. to 2 P.M., drove one hour in traffic to work, did my homework before my shift, and then worked from 4 P.M. to 12 A.M. (closing time). I was a server, busboy, janitor, and sometimes bartender. Looking back, I wonder how I survived the chaos of it all. I think I owe my survival to butter wings.

Butter wings were one of the bestselling items on the restaurant menu. The idea of it is so bizarre. I mean, how are you going to deep-fry chicken wings (already bad for your health), and then stir-fry them with a gigantic glob of butter and vegetables? I guess the vegetables cancel out all of the cholesterol in the oil and butter? Makes sense to me.

I genuinely think this is one of the best fried chicken recipes in existence. The chicken is extremely crispy. It's garlicky, a bit spicy, and provides a wonderful burst of flavor with every. single. bite. It's so good that after I finish the wings, I find myself sucking on the bones and picking at the vegetables. Am I down bad? Yes, for these wings, I am.

FOR THE CHICKEN

2½ pounds chicken party wings (about 20 pieces)

1½ tablespoons garlic powder

½ teaspoon kosher salt

½ teaspoon crushed black pepper

Vegetable or canola oil, for frying

1 cup tapioca starch

1. In a large mixing bowl, combine the chicken, garlic powder, salt, and pepper. Mix well and cover with plastic wrap. Refrigerate to marinate for at least 1 hour, or overnight.

2. To fry the chicken: Fill a heavy-bottomed pot or Dutch oven with 2 inches vegetable oil and bring to 325°F over medium heat. Meanwhile, place the tapioca starch in a wide bowl or on a plate and coat half the chicken wings thoroughly with the starch. Tap each wing against the side of the bowl to allow excess starch to fall off.

3. When the oil reaches 325°F, fry the coated chicken wings for 5 minutes. Using a strainer or tongs, carefully remove the wings from the oil and set aside. Coat the remaining wings with the tapioca starch right before you fry them. Allow the oil to come back up to temperature between batches and avoid crowding the pot.

1 tablespoon avocado oil

**⅔ small yellow onion, cut
into 1-inch squares**

**1 red bell pepper, cut into
1-inch squares**

**1 orange bell pepper, cut
into 1-inch squares**

1 jalapeño chile, sliced

½ teaspoon kosher salt

**4 tablespoons unsalted
butter**

12 garlic cloves, minced

**1 tablespoon red pepper
flakes, plus more to taste**

**2 teaspoons chicken
bouillon powder
(preferably Totole brand)**

¾ teaspoon kosher salt

¼ teaspoon MSG (optional)

**Chopped fresh cilantro
(about 2 tablespoons) and
more red pepper flakes, for
serving**

4. Once all the wings are fried, turn up the heat to medium-high and bring the oil to 375°F. Working in two batches, fry the chicken wings again, until golden brown and crispy, 4 to 5 minutes per batch. Set aside on a paper towel–lined plate.

5. For the veggies, heat the avocado oil in a wok or large pan over medium heat. Once the oil is hot, add the onion, bell peppers, and jalapeño and season with salt. Mix well and sauté until the vegetables are slightly cooked, about 2 minutes. Transfer to a plate and set aside.

6. In the same wok, melt the butter over medium heat. Add the garlic and cook until fragrant, about 30 seconds. Add the chicken, along with the stir-fried vegetables, the pepper flakes, chicken bouillon, salt, and MSG (if using). Stir-fry until all of the ingredients are thoroughly combined, about 1 minute.

7. Transfer to a serving tray/plate. Top with fresh cilantro and more red pepper flakes. Enjoy!

NOTE: *Chicken party wings are chicken wings that have been separated into flats and drumettes. If you can only find whole wings, separate them beforehand and discard the tips.*

Buffalo Wings,
page 44

Fish Sauce Wings,
page 42

Butter Wings,
page 38

FISH SAUCE WINGS

SERVES 2 TO 3

Fish sauce wings are one of the Top 3 Wing Flavors of All Time. "But what about garlic Parmesan and lemon pepper?!"—Borrrrringggg. You might be thinking . . . *Fish sauce?* I want my wings to taste like chicken, not a damn fish!

Fish sauce is essential to a lot of East Asian and Southeast Asian cuisines. It's savory, salty, umami, and—as the name implies—fishy. But what I noticed is that a lot of non-Asians' issue with it isn't the taste, but more so its smell. The good thing is, nobody is asking you to drink it straight up like it's a tequila shot. Like any other ingredient, it's supposed to be used in combination with a bunch of others.

In this recipe, we use fish sauce with sugar for extra sweetness, lime for sour and acidity, and makrut lime leaves. Makrut lime leaves are the dried leaves of makrut limes, and they add another layer of citrus flavor to our wings. They can typically be found in the refrigerated vegetable section at Asian grocery stores, especially Thai and Vietnamese stores. I got this idea from my friend Justin's mom, who is actually friends with my mom (they went to the same cosmetology school over 25 years ago before they had kids). Crazy coincidence that their kids turned out to be friends.

I like to think that these fish sauce wings are the answer to the West's lemon pepper wings. Oftentimes, I think lemon pepper flavoring is too damn strong. I'll bite into a wing sometimes and my face will swell up like I'm eating a warhead. It's too much. These fish sauce wings are crispy, umami, slightly salty, and sweet—but more importantly they have just the right amount of citrus flavor. Did I mention that they're also topped with a buttload of fried garlic? Don't let the name throw you off, because I think you'll end up liking it more than you think.

FOR THE CHICKEN

2 pounds chicken party wings (about 16 pieces)

1½ tablespoons garlic powder

¾ teaspoon kosher salt

¾ teaspoon freshly ground black pepper

Canola or vegetable oil, for frying

1 cup tapioca starch

FOR THE SAUCE

3 tablespoons sugar

1 tablespoon water

1 tablespoon lime juice

1½ tablespoons fish sauce

6 large makrut lime leaves, stems removed, thinly julienned

FOR TOPPING

¼ cup Fried Garlic (page 193), about 8 cloves

3 tablespoons chopped fresh chives

1 Thai chile, cut into thin slices (I usually do this with scissors)

1. For the chicken, in a large mixing bowl, combine the chicken, garlic powder, salt, and black pepper. Mix well and cover with plastic wrap. Refrigerate to marinate for at least 1 hour, or overnight.

2. Fill a heavy-bottomed pot or Dutch oven with 2 inches of oil and bring to 325°F over medium heat. Meanwhile, place the tapioca starch in a wide bowl or on a plate and coat half the chicken wings thoroughly with the starch. Tap each wing against the side of the bowl to allow excess starch to fall off.

3. When the oil reaches 325°F, fry the coated chicken wings for 5 minutes. Using a strainer or tongs, carefully remove the wings from the oil and set aside on a paper towel–lined plate. Coat the remaining wings with the tapioca starch right before you fry them. Allow the oil to come back up to temperature between batches and avoid crowding the pot.

4. Once all the wings are fried, turn up the heat to medium-high and bring the oil to 375°F. Working in batches, fry the chicken wings again, until golden brown and crispy, 4 to 5 minutes per batch. Set aside in a large mixing bowl.

5. For the sauce, in a medium saucepan, combine the sugar, water, lime juice, and fish sauce. Cook over medium heat until the sugar has dissolved and the sauce has thickened slightly, about 4 minutes. Add the lime leaves and continue to reduce the sauce until it is thick enough to coat the back of a spoon, about 2 additional minutes.

6. Transfer the sauce to the large mixing bowl with the fried wings and add half the fried garlic and chives. Mix well and transfer to a large serving plate. Top with the rest of the fried garlic, chives, and freshly sliced Thai chile. Serve and enjoy!

BUFFALO WINGS

SERVES 2 TO 3

Buffalo wings. Ah . . . the chicken responsible for my fried chicken addiction. It all started when my mom came home from her weekly Costco haul, when she'd buy enough food to feed an entire village. As she opened the door to our mobile home, she would yell at me to help her unload the groceries and carry them into the house. Having to stop playing my beloved game of MapleStory, I would listen to her request, annoyed. However, my mood would turn into pure happiness when I saw a gigantic pack of frozen buffalo wings peeking out of one of the grocery bags.

Buffalo wings are one of the most iconic wings of all time, which is why I had to include them in this book. These wings are double fried and then tossed in a delicious buffalo sauce made from an emulsion of your favorite hot sauce, brown sugar, and butter! It's tangy, slightly sweet, and has just a touch of spice.

2 pounds chicken party wings (about 16 wings)

2 teaspoons kosher salt

Vegetable or canola oil, for frying

⅓ cup hot sauce

1 tablespoon brown sugar

4 tablespoons cold unsalted butter, cut into small cubes

2 tablespoons finely minced fresh parsley

1. Pat the wings dry, place on a wire rack set in a baking sheet, and season on both sides with salt. Refrigerate, uncovered, for at least 12 hours, or up to 24. This will dry out the chicken skin and make the wings even crispier. (If you are in a rush, skip the refrigerator drying. Just ensure the wings are completely dry and season with salt right before frying.)

2. Pat the wings dry one last time. In a medium pot, heat 2 inches of oil to 320°F. Fry half the wings until they turn a pale yellow color, about 6 minutes. Using a strainer or tongs, carefully remove the wings from the oil and set aside on a paper towel–lined plate. Repeat with the remaining wings.

3. Bring the oil up to 375°F, then fry the wings again in two separate batches, until golden and crispy, 3 to 4 minutes. Return to the paper towel–lined plate and keep warm in a low oven.

4. In a small saucepan, combine the hot sauce and brown sugar. Bring to just below a simmer over medium heat, then remove from the heat. Slowly incorporate the cold butter, adding in a few cubes at a time while mixing. Repeat until no more butter is left and the sauce is smooth.

5. Transfer the wings to a large mixing bowl. Add buffalo sauce to your liking, along with the parsley. Toss well.

6. Serve hot and enjoy with a side of ranch and veggies, such as celery and carrots.

NASHVILLE HOT CHICKEN WINGS

SERVES ABOUT 2

I waited two hours in line to see my love—Nashville hot chicken wings.

It was the summer of 2017 when I found myself in the plaza of Chinatown, Los Angeles, for Howlin' Ray's hot chicken. The sun was blazing hot and I was sweaty, in line behind over 100 people, waiting for what Los Angeles called its best Nashville hot chicken. I hate when I want to try a popular food place and other people have the same idea as me. Ughhh, copycats: Am I right? I was absolutely miserable but was overpowered by my desire to try this foreign style of hot chicken for the first time.

Nashville hot chicken is chicken that is marinated in seasoned buttermilk, fried, and then brushed with a "paste" created from a bunch of spices mixed with the oil that you fried the chicken in. It's an absolute masterpiece. One of my biggest goals is to take a trip to Nashville and find out what authentic Nashville hot chicken tastes like. But for now, this recipe will hold me over.

NEWT

2 cups buttermilk

¼ cup hot sauce

2 tablespoons garlic powder

1 tablespoon onion powder

2 teaspoons kosher salt

1 tablespoon cayenne pepper

1 teaspoon freshly ground black pepper

1½ pounds chicken party wings (10 to 12 wings)

Vegetable or canola oil, for frying

1½ cups all-purpose flour

1. Combine the buttermilk and hot sauce in a large bowl. In a small bowl, combine the garlic powder, onion powder, salt, cayenne, and black pepper and mix well. Add half of the seasoning mix to the buttermilk and mix well. (The rest is for the flour later.)

2. Add the chicken wings to the buttermilk and stir together. Cover with plastic wrap and refrigerate for at least 6 hours, or overnight.

3. When ready to fry, fill a heavy-bottomed pot or Dutch oven with about 2 inches of vegetable oil and heat to 350°F.

4. Place the flour and the reserved seasonings in a large ziplock bag and shake together. One by one, remove half the chicken wings from the buttermilk, lifting each up and allowing excess buttermilk to drip off, and drop into the flour bag. Close the bag and shake well until the chicken is evenly coated in flour.

HOT OIL

2 teaspoons garlic powder

2 teaspoons brown sugar

½ teaspoon kosher salt

½ teaspoon onion powder

½ teaspoon smoked paprika

½ teaspoon cayenne pepper

5. Fry the coated chicken wings in the oil until golden and crispy, 8 to 9 minutes. Using a strainer or tongs, carefully remove the wings from the oil and transfer to a wire rack set in a baking sheet. Bring the oil back up to 350°F. Repeat with the remaining wings, coating them with flour just before frying. Reserve ⅓ cup of the frying oil.

6. For the hot oil, in a heatproof bowl or Pyrex measuring cup, combine the garlic powder, brown sugar, salt, onion powder, paprika, and cayenne. Add the reserved ⅓ cup of the frying oil and stir together. Immediately brush the crispy hot chicken wings with the spiced oil and enjoy!

POPCORN CHICKEN

SERVES 3 TO 4

Taiwanese popcorn chicken is one of the only types of boneless fried chicken that I tolerate. When I was growing up, my home was located relatively close to this small, family-owned boba shop that also sold popcorn chicken. It was sold as a combo: For less than ten dollars, you could get a boba with fresh french fries, popcorn chicken, and fried basil. I remember grabbing the shaker containing a spice blend of cayenne pepper and five-spice, and just having it rain over my chicken, making it as spicy as possible. Too bad someone got stabbed in front of the shop, causing them to close down for good.

To the person responsible for that crime, I will never forgive you for closing down one of the best popcorn chicken places in San Jose. You better count your days.

With revenge,
Newton

FOR THE CHICKEN AND MARINADE

1½ pounds boneless, skinless chicken thighs, cut into 1½-inch pieces

3 tablespoons Shaoxing wine

3 tablespoons soy sauce

2 tablespoons (about 6 cloves) grated garlic

2 teaspoons sugar

1 teaspoon grated fresh ginger

1 teaspoon Chinese five-spice powder

¼ teaspoon white pepper

1. Place the chicken in a large mixing bowl and add all of the marinade ingredients. Mix thoroughly. Cover with plastic wrap and refrigerate for 30 minutes.

2. Meanwhile, for the spicy seasoning: Combine all of the ingredients in a small bowl and mix together.

3. Fill a Dutch oven, heavy pot, or wok with 1½ to 2 inches of oil and heat to 375°F over medium heat.

4. Dredge half of the marinated chicken pieces in the sweet potato starch, shaking and tapping each piece to get rid of excess starch. Fry until the chicken reaches an internal temperature of 165°F, 4 to 5 minutes. Drain on a wire rack set in a baking sheet.

5. Bring the oil back up to 375°F. Dredge the second batch of chicken in the potato starch and fry until the chicken reaches an internal temperature of 165°F, about 5 minutes. Drain on the rack with the first batch. While the chicken is hot, season to taste with the spicy seasoning.

FOR THE SPICY SEASONING

2 teaspoons gochugaru (Korean pepper flakes)

1½ teaspoons cayenne

¾ teaspoon kosher salt

½ teaspoon sugar

½ teaspoon garlic powder

½ teaspoon paprika

½ teaspoon Chinese five-spice powder

¼ teaspoon MSG

FRYING AND GARNISH

Canola or vegetable oil

1 cup sweet potato starch

About 1 cup fresh Thai basil leaves

6. Flash-fry the Thai basil for 30 seconds in the hot oil. (Be careful! The oil will splutter a lot, since basil contains a bit of moisture. Cooking it in hot oil will cause a small initial popping reaction.) Using a spider strainer, carefully remove from the oil. Top the chicken with the fried basil, serve, and enjoy!

FREE GAME

Coat the chicken with the starch right before you fry or the starch will get gummy. I fry the chicken in two batches and coat half the chicken at a time.

CHICKEN KATSU

SERVES 4

Chicken katsu always puts a smile on my face because it brings me back to simpler times. In high school, I loved going to L&L's Hawaiian BBQ with my friends and ordering the katsu plate. A sliced fried chicken cutlet, rice, macaroni salad, and vegetables that I never ate—what more could you ask for? Crispy on the outside, tender on the inside.

Back then, we didn't really have much money so sometimes we would each pitch in two to four dollars and get one order, then share. Even though we only had two or three pieces each, it was worth it. But now? I can make this all for myself, muahahaha!

4 boneless, skinless chicken thighs (about 1⅓ pounds)

1 tablespoon garlic powder

1 tablespoon onion powder

1 tablespoon kosher salt

½ cup all-purpose flour

2 large eggs

2 cups panko breadcrumbs

Canola or vegetable oil, for frying

Tonkatsu sauce, for serving (optional)

White rice, for serving (optional)

Mac Salad (page 6), for serving (optional)

1. Dry the chicken thighs on both sides with paper towels. If your thighs exceed ½ inch in thickness, pound them evenly with a meat tenderizer until every part of the thigh is less than ½ inch thick. Season the chicken on both sides with the garlic powder, onion powder, and salt.

2. Set up three different plates or wide bowls for the flour, beaten eggs, and panko breadcrumbs. Coat the outside of each chicken thigh with flour, then egg, then panko. Take the time to press on the panko, to prevent any "bald spots" from appearing when frying the chicken.

3. Heat about ¾ inch of oil in a large pan over medium heat to 350°F. Fry the chicken in two batches until the internal temperature of the chicken reaches 165°F, 2 to 3 minutes on each side. Remove from the oil and drain on a wire rack set in a baking sheet.

4. Serve with tonkatsu sauce, white rice, or mac salad.

FREE GAME

While frying, I like to baste the hot oil over the top of the chicken. This allows the chicken to have a more even color throughout, resulting in a more beautiful end product.

For an Asian family, there's not many foods that we eat without chopsticks. After all, it is our main eating utensil. Eating noodles? Chopsticks. Do you want some rice? Chopsticks. Drinking water? Sa—okay, maybe not. But you get the point. It wasn't until I started going out to eat with my friends that I was introduced to different foods that are eaten with your hands.

For this chapter, we're retiring chopsticks and any other utensils. Sometimes, it's nice to be able to simply pick up food with your hands and just take a bite. Really feel the ingredients out and become one with them. One of my favorite recipes in this chapter is the Carne Asada Crispy Tacos, my re-creation of an offering from a super popular taco truck in my hometown. It wasn't until I posted a video making these that my Mexican fan base corrected me and said they're actually just tostadas. I can't believe the taco truck did me so dirty by calling them the wrong name.

4

PUT DOWN THE CHOPSTICKS

GRILLED CHEESE

SERVES 1

When it comes to grilled cheese, the possibilities are endless. From the selection of the bread to the dozens of types of cheese out there, how can you possibly make up your mind? It's impossible!

Having conducted many scientific experiments and tested dozens of grilled cheeses, I've come up with what I think is the ultimate grilled-cheese configuration of all time. Let me explain:

Sourdough: because it looks cool, has a tinge of tangy flavor, and is fancier than white bread

Gouda: nutty notes

Sharp cheddar: strong, salty flavor

Monterey Jack: stretchy goodness

Kewpie mayo: highly spreadable and browns the bread nicely

Butter: because butter, duhhhh

¼ cup (1 ounce) shredded gouda cheese

¼ cup (1 ounce) shredded sharp cheddar cheese

¼ cup (1 ounce) shredded Monterey jack cheese

1 tablespoon Kewpie mayonnaise

2 large slices sourdough bread

½ tablespoon salted butter, softened

1. In a medium mixing bowl, combine the cheeses. Using a butter knife, spread Kewpie mayonnaise on one side of each slice of bread.

2. Heat a large pan over medium-low heat. Place the bread slices, mayo side down, in the pan. Using a spoon or knife, spread a thin layer of butter over each slice. Top one slice with the cheese mixture. Top the cheese with the other slice of bread, mayo side up. Continue to cook, flipping every minute, until both sides are golden and crispy and the cheese has fully melted, 4 to 5 minutes. Enjoy!

SPAM MUSUBI

MAKES 8 SPAM MUSUBIS

Spam Musubi is the most important recipe to me because it signifies an era in my life that changed me forever. Growing up poor, I was never able to have nice things and my clothes were secondhand from the flea market. But that wasn't really an issue until high school. High school is every poor person's nightmare, because it's a mix of people like me and people with wealthy parents who can afford to buy them the nicest things—shoes, cars, you name it. I felt guilty asking my parents for new things. Partly because I knew their financial situation and felt they'd sacrificed enough for my sister and me.

So, I decided I wanted to sell Spam musubi at school. Spam musubis are these little Hawaiian snacks: rice and a slice of BBQ-sauced Spam wrapped with a strip of nori (seaweed). At the time, my mom was unemployed, so she came up with this Spam musubi recipe that would later evolve into a whole system. Every day after school, we would make eighty Spam musubis. I'd come home and she would have already fried all the pieces of Spam and cooked a giant pot of rice. I was responsible for saucing the Spam and then we would sit at our small wooden coffee table for hours, assembling Spam musubis. In the morning, we packed them up and two of my friends helped me sell them throughout the school day—and they sold like *hotcakes*. People even came from different high schools to buy my Spam musubis. And I was given the name Spam King at my school.

Despite it being a laborious process that took hours, we did it whether we were tired or not. On days that I was busy with homework or studying, Mom would work extra hard and make them herself. I used the money we made to buy myself clothes, treat my parents to dinners, and save for college.

Watching my mom taught me what it means to actually work hard and apply yourself to reach your goals. It also taught me that if you love someone, you should be selfless and willing to sacrifice your time to help them achieve their goals as well. Luckily, I don't have to sell Spam musubis anymore to afford the nice things I want, and neither does my mom. So as long as I'm alive, she's set.

recipe continues

FOR THE RICE

1 cup sweet rice

1 cup jasmine rice

3 cups warm water

1 tablespoon rice vinegar

1½ tablespoons sugar

FOR THE SAUCE AND SPAM

2 tablespoons store-bought Korean BBQ marinade (see Note)

2 tablespoons hickory smoke BBQ sauce, or your preferred smoky BBQ sauce

1 teaspoon oyster sauce

2½ teaspoons light brown sugar

½ teaspoon rice vinegar

Splash of sesame oil

One 12-ounce can reduced-fat Spam

3 sheets roasted seaweed sheets (nori), each cut into 3 even strips (about 2½ inches wide)

Furikake, to taste

Special equipment: rectangular Spam musubi mold (see Free Game)

1. Combine the sweet rice and jasmine rice in the bowl of a rice cooker. Wash well by covering with warm water and using your hands to agitate the rice. The water should turn cloudy. Drain the water, and repeat this process until the water runs clear. Drain all of the water and put the bowl back into the rice cooker. Fill with the 3 cups warm water, stir in the rice vinegar and sugar, and cook following your rice cooker's directions.

2. For the sauce, while the rice is cooking, combine all the sauce ingredients in a small mixing bowl.

3. Set the spam on its side and cut lengthwise into eight equally thick pieces. Heat a large nonstick pan over medium heat. Cook the Spam slices in the dry pan, flipping halfway through, until nice and crispy on the outsides, about 4 minutes. Reduce the heat to low, add the sauce to the pan, and stir so that the Spam is covered in the sauce. Continue cooking, flipping the Spam occasionally and allowing the sauce to reduce and caramelize on the Spam, about 5 minutes. Remove from the heat.

4. To assemble, place a strip of seaweed on a plate. Place your Spam musubi mold crosswise in the middle of the seaweed strip, add about ½ cup rice to the mold, and spread it evenly with a spoon. Using the top piece of the mold, press down to pack the rice.

5. Top the rice with furikake, to taste, and a slice of Spam. Remove the musubi mold and fold both ends of the seaweed on top of each other. Seal the ends with water and transfer to a serving plate. Repeat with the remaining seaweed, rice, and Spam. Serve and enjoy!

NOTE: *Korean BBQ marinade is available at most Asian grocery stores.*

FREE GAME

Spam musubi makers are available on Amazon or at Japanese markets. If you don't have a mold, you can make one by carefully cutting an empty Spam can horizontally in half with a saw. Cover the edges with heavy-duty tape.

SALMON CRISPY RICE

MAKES 16 PIECES

Go to any upscale restaurant in Los Angeles, and I guarantee you they'll have some sort of fish with crispy rice on the menu. Then they'll proceed to sell you two pieces for twenty dollars. HUHHH? But I'm not mad at the restaurant—rent is due, baby.

But have no fear—I'm here to make sure you don't do the same. You can make this amazing dish at home, for cheaper. I'd honestly recommend making it on a night that you're hanging out with your friends, because this finger food is meant to be shared. The hardest part is waiting for the rice to harden to a block before you fry it. The rest is a piece of cake.

Sushi-grade salmon is chopped into small pieces, mixed with a spicy mayo for a bit of heat, then placed on top of rectangles of crispy rice that is soft and sweet on the inside, while a sprinkle of lime zest helps cut through the fattiness of the salmon. This dish not only plays with different textures, but complementing flavor notes as well.

1½ cups sweet rice (alternatively, you can use sushi rice, but it won't look as pretty)

1½ cups warm water

1 tablespoon sugar

¼ teaspoon kosher salt

2 teaspoons sesame oil

2 teaspoons rice vinegar

⅓ cup vegetable or canola oil, for frying

1. Place the sweet rice in the bowl of a rice cooker. Wash well by covering with warm water and using your hands to agitate the rice. The water should turn cloudy. Drain the water, and repeat this process until the water runs clear. Drain the rice thoroughly and transfer to a rice cooker. Add the 1½ cups warm water and cook following your rice cooker's directions. When the rice is done cooking, add the sugar, salt, sesame oil, and vinegar and mix together well. Allow to cool for 5 minutes.

2. Line a 9x6-inch baking sheet (⅛ sheet tray) with plastic wrap. Place the rice on top and, using a spatula, flatten into an even layer that fills the baking sheet. Cover with more plastic wrap and place another baking sheet on top and weight it with any heavy objects that you can find to place on top. This will help to compact the rice. Refrigerate overnight. (If you are in a rush, you can blast it in the freezer for 30 minutes to an hour, until firm.)

3. Remove the rice from the tray and transfer to a cutting board. Throw away the plastic wrap and trim the edges of

recipe continues

8 ounces salmon sashimi (see Note)

2 tablespoons sriracha

2 tablespoons Kewpie mayo

1½ teaspoons lime juice

1 teaspoon soy sauce

1 tablespoon finely sliced fresh chives

FOR ASSEMBLY AND GARNISH

1 tablespoon ponzu sauce, plus more for serving

Grated lime zest, to taste

Black sesame seeds, to taste

1 serrano chile, sliced thin

the rice block, so that it is perfectly rectangular. Cut the rice block lengthwise three times into four equal strips, and then crosswise three times to make 16 equal small rectangles.

4. Heat the oil in a large nonstick pan over medium-high heat. Add half of the rice rectangles and cook on all sides until slightly golden and crispy, 2 to 3 minutes for the top and bottom, and 30 seconds for each side. (The cooking time depends on how crispy you like your rice! I prefer the rice to be slightly crispy but still chewy on the inside, so I cook it for around 2 minutes each side.) Transfer the crispy rice to a paper towel–lined plate. Repeat with the remaining rice.

5. For the salmon, mince the salmon very finely into about ⅛-inch pieces. Add to a mixing bowl, along with the sriracha, mayonnaise, lime juice, and soy sauce. Mix well. Lastly, add the chives and give it one last stir.

6. To assemble, using a brush, brush a thin layer of ponzu sauce on each piece of crispy rice. Top each piece with about 2 heaping teaspoons of the salmon mixture and finish off with lime zest, sesame seeds, and a slice of serrano chile.

7. Serve with more ponzu sauce if desired. Enjoy!

NOTE: *"Sushi grade" is a term to refer to salmon that is safe to consume raw. It is available at most Korean and Japanese markets. They're typically located near (but separate from) the fish section. Sushi-grade salmon is always packaged in plastic tins and can sometimes be labeled as salmon sashimi.*

LOBSTER ROLLS

MAKES 2 LOBSTER ROLLS

Buttery lobster in a toasted roll? Yeah, I'll have three, please. But if you're my doctor reading this, um, I'm only having one.

I was 22 years old when I had my first lobster roll. I grew up poor, bro—I rarely ever had lobster at all. *cries* While pricey, lobster rolls are really easy to make, and even easier to eat in 30 seconds. Our naturally sweet lobster meat gets coated in butter, seasoned with Old Bay, then combined with a soft brioche bun that's toasted on both sides for a crispy exterior? Holy shit.

One of my favorite things about cooking is that I can give experiences to people— especially my parents. Because they were busy raising my sister and me, they weren't able to experience lobster rolls until, when I was just starting to cook, I made the rolls for the first time. I remember my mom driving me to a seafood market to pick out the lobster. She had a confused look on her face when we brought home lobster and hot dog buns, but she let me be. As I filmed myself poaching the lobster, picking apart its meat, and tossing it in melted butter, she became even more curious. When I was done, I made two more lobster rolls—one for Mom and one for Dad. I watched them try this American classic for the first time and saw their faces light up in satisfaction. Lobster rolls hold a special place in my heart because I was able to share this with them and repay them just a tiny bit for the sacrifices they made for me and my sister.

1 tablespoon kosher salt

Two 4-ounce lobster tails

2 brioche split-top hot dog buns

2 teaspoons Kewpie mayo

2 tablespoons unsalted butter

½ teaspoon Old Bay seasoning

¼ teaspoon celery salt

Finely chopped fresh chives, for serving

Lemon wedges and chips, for serving

1. Fill a medium pot with water, add 1 tablespoon salt, and bring to a boil. Meanwhile, prepare an ice bath by filling a medium mixing bowl with cold water and a few ice cubes.

2. When the water comes to a boil, drop in the lobster tails and cook until the internal meat temperature reaches 140°F, 3 to 3½ minutes. Transfer the lobster tails to the ice water and let sit for 30 seconds. This will stop any further cooking, so that the lobster meat won't be a rubbery mess. Drain the tails and transfer to a cutting board.

3. Prepare the buns by slicing a bit of the crust off the outer sides. I do this to create more surface area for a crispier texture when toasted. If your buns are already "raw" on the sides, skip this step.

recipe continues

NEWT

4. Spread a thin layer of Kewpie mayo on both sides of each bun half. Toast in a pan over medium heat, until golden brown on both sides, 45 to 60 seconds per side. Set aside.

5. To harvest the lobster meat, cut each lobster tail shell down the middle with scissors, and pull out the meat. Make an incision down the middle of the tail meat, and remove any visible digestive tract (the black veiny thing). Once the meat is cleaned, cut it into bite-size pieces.

6. Melt the butter in a pan over low heat. Add the lobster meat, season with Old Bay and celery salt, and heat through until warm, about 45 seconds.

7. Remove from the heat and divide the lobster meat between the two buns. Spoon the remaining butter in the pan over the lobster rolls. Top with the chopped chives and serve with a few wedges of lemon and handfuls of chips.

MUSSELS IN TOMATO SAUCE WITH TOASTED SOURDOUGH

SERVES 2

2 tablespoons olive oil

3 tablespoons minced shallot (from 1 small shallot)

2 tablespoons minced garlic (from 6 medium cloves)

1 tablespoon tomato paste

1½ teaspoons Calabrian chili paste (see sidebar)

1 teaspoon ground fennel seeds

¼ cup dry white wine

⅓ cup seafood stock (see Note), or vegetable stock

One 14.5-ounce can diced roasted tomatoes

1 tablespoon lemon juice

1 tablespoon unsalted butter

1 tablespoon sugar

½ teaspoon MSG (optional)

Kosher salt, to taste

1 pound unopened mussels, cleaned and debearded (see Free Game)

3 tablespoons chopped fresh parsley, plus more for serving

Olive Oil–Toasted Sourdough Bread (recipe follows)

Lemon wedges, for serving

No matter what Italian restaurant I end up at, I always order some form of mussels with bread—no questions asked. I find that eating shellfish like mussels and clams is so satisfying. I think it's because the meat is connected to its shell, which serves as its own natural delivery vehicle that is on standby—awaiting my directions to be delivered straight into my mouth. Am I being weird? Does this make sense to anyone else? No? Okay well . . .

There's typically two versions of mussel dishes that you can find at restaurants. One is with a creamy white wine sauce, and the other is with a tomato sauce. And the tomato is going to do it for me every time. This broth is tomatoey (duh), garlicky, spicy, and the perfect amount of sweet. Pair with pieces of sourdough toasted in olive oil to deliver an absolute flavor bomb of bite. My favorite part is that most of the work is in prepping our ingredients. The work lies in making sure the mussels are properly cleaned, free of debris, and debearded (pulling out those hairs sticking out of the shell). The actual dish itself comes together in less than 10 minutes.

1. Heat the olive oil in a large lidded pan over medium-low heat. Add the shallot and garlic and sauté until fragrant and starting to soften, about 1 minute. Add the tomato paste, chili paste, and ground fennel and continue to sauté for another minute, until well incorporated.

2. Raise the heat to medium and add the white wine. Bring to a boil, stirring and scraping the bottom and sides of the pan with a rubber spatula or a wooden spoon to deglaze. Let the alcohol cook off, about 1 minute, then add the stock, tomatoes, lemon juice, butter, sugar, and MSG (if using). I like

recipe continues

to use a potato masher to break up the chunks of tomato into smaller pieces. Season with salt and bring to a simmer.

3. Add the cleaned mussels to the simmering tomato mixture, toss well, and cover with a lid. Cook for 5 minutes or so. Any mussels that aren't open after cooking should be discarded. Add the parsley and give the mixture one last stir before serving with toasted sourdough, lemon wedges, and more parsley.

NOTE: *I usually order my seafood stock ready-made from my local grocery store. Many stores that sell seafood will have stock on hand to sell.*

OLIVE OIL—TOASTED SOURDOUGH BREAD

1 loaf crusty sourdough bread
Olive oil, to taste
1 garlic clove, cut in half

1. Slice the bread into ¾-inch-thick pieces and drizzle both sides of the slices generously with olive oil.

2. Toast in a skillet over medium heat, flipping the slices over until nicely colored on both sides. Once toasted, rub with the cut sides of the garlic pieces.

FREE GAME

To clean mussels, remove from the plastic bag and refrigerate until ready to cook. Begin by running them under cold water in a colander. Use a brush to brush off any sand and debris from the shells. A mussel that is open should be tapped against a surface to see if it closes up. If it closes, it's still alive and safe to eat. If it doesn't close up, discard (it's dead). Mussels have beards (the hair-like fibers that stick outside the shell). Remove by yanking on them, pulling towards the foot of the mussel (where the shells are attached).

CALABRIAN CHILI PASTE

Calabrian chili paste is a spicy Southern Italian condiment made from chiles that are native to Calabria, the "toe" of the Italian boot. The chiles are dried and crushed with olive oil. Salt and vinegar are sometimes added. It is typically sold in jars and is easy to find in Italian delis, online, and even at some Trader Joe's!

CARNE ASADA CRISPY TACOS (TECHNICALLY, TOSTADAS)

SERVES 4

In San Jose, there's a specific taco truck that is pretty much our national monument. Well, at least for my generation. Yes, I'm talking about none other than the Spartan Tacos. Spartan Tacos is the Mexican food truck that parks in the parking lot of an auto-body shop in Downtown San Jose.

I can't tell you all the times my friends and I would end up there at midnight, completely drunk out of our minds, yearning for a "pick-me-up." I remember my order clearly too. Crispy carne asada tacos with pico de gallo, mango salsa, and their orange sauce. When ordering, I even remembered to roll my R's, just so that I didn't sound unseasoned.

The feeling of eating these tacos was like I had died and come back to life—a true out-of-body experience. I loved Spartan Tacos so much that I've pretty much taken every person I know there. Since not everyone lives near a Spartan Taco truck, this is a recipe to replicate the experience at home. Though, not nearly as good. Full disclaimer: I call these Crispy Tacos because that's what we know them as in San Jose, but they're technically tostadas. Tostadas and tacos differ in the fact that in the former, the tortilla is deep-fried or toasted.

FOR THE MARINADE

½ **bunch fresh cilantro, about 2 cups leaves and upper stems**

5 **garlic cloves**

½ **jalapeño chile, seeded and roughly chopped**

⅓ **cup orange juice**

¼ **cup olive oil**

1 **tablespoon lime juice**

2 **teaspoons ground cumin**

2 **teaspoons dried oregano**

2 **teaspoons kosher salt**

½ **teaspoon ground pepper**

1. Combine all of the marinade ingredients in a food processor and blend until the garlic and jalapeño are reduced to a small mince, about 30 seconds.

2. Place the meat in a gallon-size ziplock bag and add all of the marinade. Close the bag and press out as much air as possible. Give the bag a couple of good shakes to ensure that the meat is completely covered in the marinade. Transfer to the fridge and marinate for anywhere from 6 to 24 hours.

3. When ready to cook, heat a cast-iron skillet over medium-high heat. Add 1 tablespoon of the avocado oil and wait until it begins to smoke. Then add half the marinated steak and cook until it has a nice sear, 2 to 3 minutes on each side. Transfer to a bowl and repeat with the remaining oil and meat.

recipe continues

FOR THE MEAT

1½ pounds skirt steak or flank steak, trimmed and cut into 3-inch-wide slabs

2 tablespoons avocado oil

Vegetable or canola oil, for frying

12 street taco–size corn tortillas

FOR ASSEMBLY

1 cup Pico de Gallo (page 187)

¾ cup Orange Salsa (page 190)

Crema or sour cream, to taste (optional)

Minced fresh cilantro, to taste

4. Using a sharp knife, cut the steak into small (about ¼-inch) cubes. You don't need to be precise, just cut them into small bits. Return the skillet to medium-high heat and, when just about smoking, return all of the meat and continue cooking until it's charred to your liking, 1 to 2 minutes. Set aside.

5. Heat ½ inch vegetable oil in a small skillet to 350°F. Fry one tortilla until golden and crispy, about 30 seconds per side (flip using tongs or a skimmer). Drain on a paper towel. Repeat with remaining tortillas. If desired, sprinkle the crispy tortillas with salt.

6. To assemble the tacos, set out four plates and place three fried tortillas on each plate. Distribute the meat evenly on each tortilla. Top with pico de gallo, orange salsa, crema (if using), and cilantro. Enjoy!

QUESABIRRIA TACOS

MAKES ABOUT 24 TACOS

Quesabirria tacos are one of those culinary discoveries that just push the entire human race forward. It's a movement and a cultural phenomenon. Prior to knowing about it, my choice of meat for tacos was carne asada or al pastor. It wasn't until quesabirria tacos became a viral food trend on Instagram that I questioned where they've been all my life and why one wasn't in my mouth.

It starts with birria, a Mexican meat stew that is cooked with a bunch of herbs and spices. Over time, the meat gets cooked to the point where it just falls apart in your hands, which is one of the most satisfying feelings ever.

Assemble the tacos by transferring this delicate beef to a corn tortilla that's been dipped in the braising liquid. Top it with onions, cilantro, and shredded Oaxaca cheese, fold it over, and get a quick sear to crisp up the outsides of the tortilla. Before consuming, dip the tacos back into the consommé (braising liquid), and take a bite of the most juicy, succulent, toe-curling taco you've ever had in your life. You're welcome.

FOR THE BRAISING LIQUID BASE

8 dried guajillo chiles

5 dried chiles de arbol

2 dried ancho chiles

2 tablespoons avocado oil

1 white onion, chopped

3 Roma tomatoes, quartered, cored, and seeded

12 garlic cloves, peeled and lightly smashed

½ teaspoon kosher salt

2 cups water

1 tablespoon white vinegar

4 whole cloves

1. For the braising liquid base: Prepare the dried chiles by removing the stems and seeds. Place in a heatproof bowl and cover with hot water. Set aside for 30 minutes, while you prepare the vegetables. (Soaking the chiles will rehydrate them and make them softer and easier to blend later on.)

2. Heat the oil in a medium frying pan over medium heat. Add the white onion, tomatoes, and garlic, season with salt, and cook until the onion and tomatoes have softened and slightly charred, 8 to 10 minutes. Remove from the heat and transfer to a blender.

3. Drain the chiles and add to the blender, along with the remaining braising liquid ingredients. Blend on high for 1 minute, until smooth, and set aside.

4. For the beef: Pat it dry with a paper towel. Heat the oil in a large pot over medium-high heat. Salt half of the beef generously, add to the pot, and brown on all sides,

recipe continues

1 teaspoon ground cumin

1 teaspoon dried thyme

1 teaspoon dried oregano

¼ teaspoon freshly ground black pepper

FOR THE BEEF

3 pounds beef chuck roast, cut into 2-inch cubes (see Note)

2 tablespoons avocado oil

Kosher salt

5 cups water

1 chicken bouillon cube (I prefer Knorr)

3 bay leaves

FOR ASSEMBLY

Avocado oil, as needed

24 street taco–size corn tortillas

10 ounces Oaxaca cheese, shredded

½ red onion, minced

1 bunch fresh cilantro, chopped

Lime wedges, for serving

1 to 2 minutes per side. Remove to a bowl or plate. Repeat with the remaining beef.

5. Return all the beef to the pot. Place a large wire mesh strainer over the pot and strain the blended chile mixture into the pot. Using a spatula, press down on the solids, taking your time to extract as much liquid as possible (as that's where all the flavor is). Discard the solids once done.

6. Add the water, chicken bouillon, and bay leaves to the pot and bring to a simmer over medium-high heat. Reduce the heat to maintain a low simmer, cover partially, and cook until the meat is fork-tender, about 3 hours. Check periodically, adding water if the braising liquid is reducing too quickly. (Don't add too much water, or else it will dilute the braising liquid/consommé. It's not the end of the world; you'll just have to boil the consommé later on to reduce it and concentrate the flavors.)

7. Transfer the beef to a heatproof bowl and shred into small pieces using two forks. Add ¼ cup of the consommé and mix well to prevent the meat from drying out.

8. To assemble the tacos: Heat a large pan over medium heat and add 1 teaspoon oil. Using your hands, dip a corn tortilla into the consommé and transfer to the pan. Top with cheese, shredded beef, red onion, and cilantro. Fold the taco in half and cook, flipping from side to side, until the taco reaches your desired crispiness on the outside. Transfer to a serving plate. Repeat to make 24 tacos.

9. Serve with lime wedges and small bowls of the consommé for dipping the tacos. Enjoy!

NOTE: *Cutting the beef into small pieces provides more surface area to brown and develop flavor.*

FREE GAME

I brown the meat in two separate batches to avoid overcrowding. Also, salting the meat right before searing it (as opposed to salting it all at once and letting some of it sit idle on the side) is important because salt draws out moisture, and the more you let the meat sit with salt, the more moisture will be drawn out. We want to brown the meat, not boil it!

FISH TACOS

MAKES 16 TACOS, SERVING ABOUT 4

When we're talking about my favorite places to eat in high school, we can't pass on Rubio's. I know what you're thinking. "Ohhhh shit. Rubio's! I totally forgot that restaurant existed." I know, right? Rubio's is that one friend that you never really talk to, but when you *do* reconnect, it's always a good time. You know what else is a good time? Rubio's fish tacos.

One of my favorite things to eat after school on Tuesdays were fish tacos. Mostly because of the two-dollar fish taco special Rubio's had. I had a routine to save money every day of the week, just so I could ditch class on Tuesday and ball out on some fish tacos. Yes—they were that good.

I'll never forget the time my friend Lawrence couldn't go home because his neighbor was in an altercation with the police. The guy literally lived at the unit next to his, and they locked down the entire block for 12 hours so he had nowhere to go. Naturally, we took him to Rubio's to get some fish tacos and hung out there for hours until everything was good again. Did the tacos make Lawrence feel any better? Probably not. But at least he had a fire meal.

FOR THE FISH

1 pound cod fillets, cut into ½-inch-thick slices

2 teaspoons garlic powder

¾ teaspoon smoked paprika

½ teaspoon kosher salt

¼ cup all-purpose flour, for dusting

1. Place the cod slices on a baking sheet and season with the garlic powder, paprika, and salt. Then dust all sides of the fillets with flour.

2. To make the batter, combine the flour, Old Bay, and baking powder in a medium mixing bowl and mix well. Slowly whisk in the beer and whisk until just combined.

3. Heat 2 inches oil in a medium pot or pan to 375°F. In small batches, dip the fish into the wet batter and place in the hot oil. Fry, flipping the fish halfway, until brown and crispy, about 3 minutes. To get the crispiest results, spoon a few more tablespoons of the wet batter on top of the fish while it's frying. Drain on a wire rack set in a baking sheet. Allow the oil to reach 375°F before continuing with each new batch.

1 cup all-purpose flour

1 tablespoon Old Bay seasoning

2 teaspoons baking powder

12 ounces cold beer, preferably an IPA

Vegetable or canola oil, for frying

FOR ASSEMBLY

16 street taco–size corn tortillas

¼ small red cabbage, thinly shredded

1 cup Pico de Gallo (page 187)

¼ cup Mexican crema, or sour cream

½ cup Orange Salsa (page 190)

Chopped fresh cilantro, to taste

Limes wedges, for serving

4. While the fish are frying, heat a large nonstick pan over medium heat for the tortillas. Place two or three tortillas in the pan, and cook until just warmed through, about 45 seconds on each side.

5. To assemble the fish tacos, lay out the warm tortillas on serving plates. Transfer a piece of fried fish onto each tortilla and top with shredded cabbage, pico de gallo, crema, orange salsa, and cilantro. Serve with lime wedges.

Like all fried foods, fish tacos are best when the fish is hot and crispy, right out of the oil. If serving guests, don't fry all your fish and try to serve (and eat) them at once. By the time the last batch of fish comes out, your initial batch will already be cold and sad. Fry and serve the tacos as you go!

SMASH BURGERS

MAKES 4 BURGERS

Why go to a fast-food burger joint to buy a smash burger when you can make it at home for cheaper, *and* have your entire living room smelling like browned beef? Free air freshener? That's what I like to call a win-win situation. Making burgers at home doesn't require much effort at all, and I guarantee you that you can make it better than any of those restaurants.

Okay, the lingering beef aroma can be off-putting, but making smash burgers is one of my favorite things to do for friends and family. Take it this way: Of all the dishes I've cooked, my dad has only ever complimented this one. In fact, I used to cook him two burgers at a time—and I'm sure he would happily eat a third one if he didn't have high cholesterol. I realized that if my Asian dad likes this dish, so will everyone else in my life. And it's true. In my second year in L.A., I moved to an apartment and was able to make friends (shocking, right?). The first meal that I cooked for everyone was these smash burgers, and they all were ecstatic about them, along with the fries and cold glasses of coke. My heart was full because I never thought I'd have so many friends who were willing to try my food.

4 burger buns, preferably brioche or King's Hawaiian

¼ cup Kewpie mayo

1 pound 80 percent lean ground beef

1 tablespoon avocado oil

1 teaspoon garlic powder

1 teaspoon kosher salt

1 teaspoon freshly ground black pepper

8 slices cheddar cheese

¼ cup Thousand Island dressing, store-bought or homemade

1 medium beefsteak tomato, cut into ⅓-inch-thick slices

1. Separate the buns and spread a thin layer of Kewpie mayo over the cut surfaces of both the tops and bottoms. Heat a large pan over medium-high heat. Working in two batches, place the buns cut side down in the pan. Use your hands or a spatula to press down on the buns to ensure they make full contact with the pan, for an even brown. Toast for about 30 seconds. Set aside, and repeat with remaining buns.

2. Divide the ground beef into eight equal portions. Using your hands, form each portion into a ball.

3. Heat a large heavy cast-iron frying pan over medium-high heat and add the avocado oil. When the oil is hot, place two beef balls in the pan, not too close to each other, and use a wide spatula or the bottom of a sauce pot to press down to make them as flat as possible. (Be really careful, as the hot oil can splatter!) Season to taste with garlic powder, salt, and pepper and cook the patties until you see browning on the edges, about 45 seconds. Flip and immediately place a slice

Maldon sea salt flakes

4 pieces butter lettuce, cut to fit the size of the buns

¼ cup Caramelized Onions (page 196)

of cheddar cheese on top of each patty. Cover the pan with a lid and cook until the cheese has melted slightly, about 30 to 45 seconds. Using a spatula, stack one patty on top of the other and transfer to a plate.

4. Repeat step 3 with the remaining balls of meat , adding more avocado oil in between batches, if necessary. As you cook the patties, you'll notice burnt bits start to form. Simply scrape them away with your spatula, and discard.

5. Assemble the burgers by spreading 1 tablespoon Thousand Island dressing on each bottom bun. Add a tomato slice and season with flaky salt, to taste. Place a lettuce leaf on top of the tomato, followed by a double burger patty, caramelized onions, and the top bun. Enjoy!

PÂTÉ CHAUD

MAKES 9 PASTRIES

Pâté chaud (pronounced *pah-teh-so*) is the one pastry that I hold dear to my heart. As a kid, my mom would bring home a pink box of these from a pastry shop, Vien Dong, near our home. Even when I got older, these pastries never got old. I'd walk home from school and stop by my local bakery just to get them. I'd get five for three dollars, gobble them on my walk home, and then be in a food coma, knocked out on the couch moments later.

Pâté chaud is a Vietnamese savory pastry that was adopted from the French. The flaky filled pastry is our version of a meat pie, where the main character is an umami filling of ground pork, surrounded by layers of flaky dough goodness. If you didn't know, the French colonized Vietnam for a period of time, which is why there're so many Vietnamese dishes that use French techniques and ingredients. You know . . . like bánh mì, coffee, escargot? The French really snapped with their cooking, huh? Anyways, screw all that. I suck at history.

Despite the name being pâté chaud, this version doesn't include pâté—or pork liver paste. Many people make it either with or without it, and since the bakeries I visited growing up didn't include pâté, I'm not going to either. Plus, I figured quite a bit of people might be uncomfortable with the thought of eating liver, and that's completely fine. My goal is to make these recipes the least intimidating that I can, so that you can be comfortable to start cooking. :)

One 17.3-ounce box frozen puff pastry dough (2 sheets)

Nonstick spray or butter for the parchment

FOR THE MEAT FILLING

8 ounces ground pork

¼ small yellow onion, minced (about ¼ cup)

1 garlic clove, minced

1½ teaspoons oyster sauce

1 teaspoon potato starch

1 teaspoon fish sauce

1. Take the pastry dough out of the freezer and let it thaw at room temperature just until it's pliable enough to work with, 30 to 45 minutes. Alternatively, you can thaw the dough overnight in the refrigerator.

2. Preheat the oven to 350°F and position a rack in the middle. Line a baking sheet with parchment paper and lightly spray with cooking oil, or brush lightly with butter.

3. Cut each dough sheet into nine even squares, about 3x3 inches each, to make 18 pieces.

4. Place all of the ingredients for the meat filling except the egg in a mixing bowl and mix until everything is just combined. Don't overmix or the filling will be too dense. It helps if you shape your mixing hand like a claw.

¾ teaspoon sugar

½ teaspoon granulated mushroom bouillon

½ teaspoon freshly ground black pepper

⅛ teaspoon (pinch) salt

1 large egg, beaten

5. Lay out nine squares of pastry. Scoop about 2 tablespoons filling onto each square, creating a half-sphere right in the middle. Brush the edges of the pastry with beaten egg, then place a remaining pastry sheet on top of each and press together with your fingers. Using a fork, press down on the outer edges of each square to seal the layers together and create an attractive border.

6. Transfer the pastries to the baking sheet and brush each with a thin layer of egg wash. Bake until golden brown, 25 to 30 minutes. Serve hot or warm.

Don't talk to me when I'm hungry. No, like literally, I'm not a fun person to be around. When I'm on an empty stomach, hanging out with me is like walking across a football field. Except, there are bombs randomly placed under the ground—like Minesweeper. One wrong move, and it wraps. I read online somewhere that hunger actually affects the part of your brain that controls your mood, so I suppose we all get hangry to some degree.

This chapter is for those who want food, and who want it now. Okay, maybe not *now*. Because in reality, if you were *that* hungry, you'd probably eat something fast, like chips or ramen noodles. These are recipes that I gravitate towards when I want to throw something together quick. The only time-consuming part would be waiting for the meat to marinate. Other than that, we're moving at the speed of light and tossing ingredients together to make a satisfying meal.

If you want to pick only one recipe out of this chapter to try, please consider the Vietnamese Shaking Beef (Bò Lúc Lắc). It's a famous and iconic Vietnamese dish that I think often gets overlooked.

5

ME HANGRY

GARLIC NOODLES

SERVES 4

Picture this. You're at a seafood boil restaurant. You have your wittle plastic bib on like a wittle baby, and you're elbows deep in two pounds of crawfish and shrimp. Your meal is going amazing (hopefully you didn't get any juices on your shirt), but something feels a little off. Is mercury in retrograde? No, that passed already. Did you forget to fold your laundry? No, your mom still does that for you. Then what could it be? Then it clicks in your mind—you forgot to order garlic noodles. You flag down the waiter to place an order and all is right in the world again.

Garlic noodles are one of the easiest things in the world to make. It's spaghetti noodles, butter, an umami-heavy sauce, and loads of garlic. It's the umami savory carb that you can eat by itself, but also goes great with almost any protein, such as Vietnamese Shaking Beef (page 102), Ginger Scallion Lobster (page 129), and more.

8 ounces spaghetti

2 tablespoons sugar

2 tablespoons oyster sauce

1 tablespoon Maggi liquid seasoning (see Note)

2 teaspoons fish sauce

3 tablespoons unsalted butter

1 scallion, sliced, white and green parts separated

10 garlic cloves, minced

½ teaspoon sesame oil

3 tablespoons freshly grated Parmesan

1. Cook the spaghetti in a large pot of boiling salted water according to package instructions.

2. While the pasta is cooking, mix the sugar, oyster sauce, Maggi, and fish sauce together in a small bowl, then set the sauce aside.

3. Melt the butter in a skillet over medium heat. Add the white part of the scallion and the garlic and cook for 45 seconds, or until fragrant.

4. When the noodles are done, drain and add them to the pan, along with the sauce. Mix well.

5. Drizzle on the sesame oil and top with the green part of the scallion. Mix one last time before taking the pan off the heat. Top with grated Parmesan, and enjoy while hot!

NOTE: *Maggi liquid seasoning is a popular ingredient used in Asian cuisine. The flavor profile is sort of like an umami soy sauce. It's readily available in most Asian grocery stores, in the same aisle as soy sauce and fish sauce.*

KIMCHI FRIED RICE

SERVES 2

I don't like kimchi. I know if you're Korean and reading this, you probably just took off your slipper and cocked your arm back to throw it at me. To be fair, I don't like the majority of pickled or fermented things. However, I *love* kimchi fried rice. Does this make any sense to anybody?

Why is kimchi fried rice one of my favorites? Well, first of all, it's rice (really good start). Secondly, it uses meat that I've been eating since growing up: Spam. (Spam is a bit controversial to most people because it's a mystery meat. There are people out there who think Spam is disgusting and claim they wouldn't touch it with a five-foot pole. To that I say, "Thank u. More for me <3.") Lastly, the way we incorporate the kimchi (browning it a bit before adding to the rice) makes it a lot less sharp and sour, which I really like.

Make sure all ingredients are prepped and ready before starting to cook. Fried rice is very quick to make, and can be stressful if you don't prepare! If you're looking for a couple ways to spice up your kimchi fried rice, I like to eat mine with roasted seaweed and a fried egg.

2 tablespoons plus ½ teaspoon avocado oil

3 cups day-old steamed white rice

Half 12-ounce can reduced-sodium Spam, cut into ½-inch cubes

1 cup kimchi, minced

⅓ yellow onion, minced (about ⅓ cup)

2 scallions, minced, white and green parts separated, green parts reserved for garnish

3 garlic cloves, minced

1 to 2 tablespoons gochujang, depending on spice preference

1 tablespoon soy sauce

1. Heat a nonstick pan or a well-seasoned wok over high heat. Add 1 tablespoon of the avocado oil, then the rice. Using a spatula, press down on the rice to break apart any of the clumps. The goal is to separate each individual grain. Stir frequently and continue cooking until the rice is no longer clumpy and adequately dry, about 2 minutes. Transfer the rice to a bowl and set aside.

2. In the same pan, stir-fry the Spam until crispy on the surface, 3 to 4 minutes. Remove from the pan and set aside.

3. Add ½ teaspoon avocado oil to the pan and the kimchi. Stir-fry until the surface is browned, 3 to 4 minutes. Transfer to the bowl with the Spam.

4. Reduce the heat to medium-high and add the remaining 1 tablespoon avocado oil to the pan. Add the onion and stir-fry until softened, about 2 minutes. Add the white parts of the scallions and the garlic and cook until fragrant, about 30 seconds.

1 teaspoon sesame oil

¼ teaspoon freshly ground black pepper

½ teaspoon sugar

Pinch of MSG (optional)

5. Return the rice to the pan and mix together well. Add the gochujang and soy sauce and continue stirring and mixing until the gochujang is evenly dispersed throughout the rice. Once that's done, return the Spam and kimchi to the pan and give everything one last toss before removing from the heat.

6. Finish with sesame oil, black pepper, sugar, and MSG (if using) and garnish with the green parts of the scallions. Adjust for salt if needed, and enjoy!

CHICKEN ADOBO

SERVES 2

I love Filipino people. Is it because they created what I think is the best fried chicken in the world, Jollibee? Yes. But also, throughout my life, I always find that Filipinos and I get along really well. From the way that we talk, joke around, trauma bond—they always make me feel comfortable and at home.

Which is why I wasn't surprised when I found out that the biggest demographic of my supporters is from the Philippines. I think it's one of those situations where the stars align perfectly, and I wouldn't have it any other way. This recipe is dedicated to all of my loving Filipino viewers. I don't know what I did to receive such great support from you guys, but I had to include a recipe of my favorite Filipino dish, chicken adobo, in this cookbook. Chicken adobo is a Filipino dish braised in a salty, acidic, and slightly sweet liquid. The beautiful thing is that it doesn't require many ingredients, and it's interpreted differently among different families as well. Some people prefer their adobo on the more "soy saucy" side, some prefer theirs to be sweeter. This is how I make mine!

I hope you take it as a sign of respect and gratitude. Mahal Kita.

1 cup water

¾ cup vinegar, preferably Datu Puti brand (see Note)

¾ cup soy sauce, preferably Silver Swan brand (see Note)

5 tablespoons brown sugar

20 garlic cloves, peeled and smashed

1 tablespoon whole black peppercorns

3 bay leaves

2 pounds chicken party wings or drumettes

2 tablespoons avocado oil, plus more as needed

1. Mix together the water, vinegar, soy sauce, brown sugar, garlic, black peppercorns, and bay leaves. Stir until the sugar has dissolved.

2. Place the chicken in a large bowl and pour on the marinade. Cover and refrigerate for at least 2 hours, or up to 3 hours. Drain the chicken but don't discard the marinade.

3. Place a Dutch oven or large heavy pot over medium-high heat and add the oil. When the oil is hot, add half the chicken wings (so you don't crowd the pan) and brown on all sides, about 1½ minutes per side. Remove to a bowl or a sheet pan. Repeat to brown the remaining chicken, adding more oil if necessary.

4. Return all of the chicken to the pot, pour in the reserved marinade, and mix well. Bring to a boil, then reduce the heat to low, cover partially, and simmer for 15 minutes. Check from time to time to make sure the liquid remains at a slow

simmer. If the mixture cooks too quickly the chicken will be tough. Adjust the heat or change to a different burner if necessary. Flip the chicken wings over and continue to cook uncovered over low heat for another 15 minutes, until the chicken is cooked all the way through and the braising liquid has reduced. Remove and discard the bay leaves. Using a skimmer, skim out any scum that may have risen to the top. Serve with white rice.

NOTE: *The most common type of vinegar in the Philippines—and what is used in adobos—is cane vinegar, made from sugar cane. Datu Puti is the brand that is most widely available in the United States. Datu Puti also makes a soy sauce that is used in Filipino dishes like this one. Silver Swan is another brand of soy sauce used in the Philippines. You can find these in most Asian markets and definitely at Filipino markets like Seafood City. They are also available on Amazon, sometimes sold as a package. The bottles are gigantic, and it even takes me, cooking every day, up to a year to use one up. In case you can't find Datu Puti brand vinegar or are in a pinch, you can substitute distilled white vinegar or apple cider vinegar.*

THAI BASIL CHICKEN (PAD KRAPOW GAI)

SERVES 2

Ground chicken and rice is the most boring meal to eat—unless it's Thai basil chicken. In that case, it's lit. Pad krapow gai is one of my favorite Thai foods. It's a bit of everything—salty, sweet, and spicy. The spice comes from Thai chili peppers, which, despite their small size, pack a mean punch. While I was working on this recipe, I had an accident when prepping the chiles. There was something in my eye that was bothering me so I quickly rubbed it. What's the problem here? I forgot to wash my hands . . . Holy crap. My eye felt like it caught on flames. The next 30 minutes consisted of me running my eyes under water, followed by tears running down my face (against my will). I've never been pepper sprayed, but this is what I would imagine it feels like. Did I learn my lesson? Yes. Will this happen again? Probably. Learn from my mistakes, and make sure you wash your hands thoroughly when dealing with Thai chili peppers.

FOR THE SAUCE

1 tablespoon oyster sauce

2 teaspoons fish sauce

1½ teaspoons dark soy sauce

1½ teaspoons soy sauce

2 teaspoons sugar

2 tablespoons water

FOR THE CHICKEN

2 tablespoons avocado oil

5 garlic cloves, minced

¼ shallot, minced
(about 1 tablespoon)

3 to 5 Thai chili peppers, sliced, or more or less to taste

½ bell pepper, finely diced

12 ounces ground chicken

¼ teaspoon kosher salt

½ teaspoon freshly ground black pepper

1½ cups Thai basil
(about ½ ounce)

FOR SERVING

Steamed white rice

2 fried eggs

1. Mix together all of the ingredients for the sauce in a small bowl and stir to dissolve the sugar. Set aside.

2. For the chicken, heat a wok over medium-high heat and add the avocado oil. Add the garlic, shallot, and Thai chilis and stir-fry for about 30 seconds, until fragrant. Add the bell pepper and stir-fry for 30 seconds, until just beginning to soften.

3. Add the ground chicken and break it apart with a spatula while you press it into the wok with the back of the spatula. Season with the salt and black pepper and stir-fry until the chicken is no longer pink, about 3 minutes.

4. Stir in the sauce, mix well, and reduce for 30 seconds before adding the basil. Give the mixture one last stir before removing from the heat. Serve the chicken over a bed of white rice and top each serving with a fried egg.

CANTONESE STEAMED FISH

SERVES 2

There's nothing that will make you feel more like a skinny legend than eating something steamed.

Cantonese steamed fish is my go-to meal when I feel like I want to get my health in order, but let's face it—is my health ever really in order? Most healthy foods taste too "clean" or "bland" to me, making them very unsatisfying. Nobody wants to be left with the feeling of emptiness after a meal. Luckily, Cantonese steamed fish tastes delicious *and* is great for you. One of the things that always draws me to the dish is how simple, but euphoric, the flavors are. The fish is surrounded by a sauce that is slightly salty but balanced by the sweetness from the sugar. My favorite part is pouring the hot oil on top of everything, releasing an intoxicating fragrance that ties everything together. Oh yeah, my personal touch is adding fried scallions to switch up the texture. Give this recipe a try to get a taste of the heaven I'm talking about.

1 pound white fish fillets
(such as cod or tilapia),
1 inch thick or less

2 teaspoons sugar

2 tablespoons hot water

3 tablespoons light soy
sauce

2-inch knob of ginger,
peeled and thinly julienned

2 scallions, thinly julienned

2 tablespoons shallot oil
(from the Fried Shallots), or
regular oil

¼ cup Fried Shallots (page
194)

1. Fill a pot with a steamer attachment with 1 inch of water and bring to a simmer. Place the fish fillets on a plate. When the water starts simmering, place the plate with the fish on top of the steamer attachment, and cover with a lid. Steam until the fish is cooked all the way through and has an internal temperature of 145°F, 4 to 8 minutes, depending on thickness. (Check the temperature of the fish periodically by sticking a meat thermometer into the thickest part.) Uncover and remove the plate with the fish. Pour off all of the liquid that has accumulated on the plate, and set the fish aside.

2. In a small mixing bowl, combine the sugar and hot water and mix until the sugar has dissolved. Add the soy sauce, mix once more, and pour the sauce over the fish. Top with the julienned ginger and scallions.

3. In a small pan, heat the shallot oil over high heat until the oil is shimmering, about 1 minute. Immediately pour the hot oil over the scallions and ginger, and top with fried shallots. Enjoy!

THAI STIR-FRIED RICE NOODLES (PAD SEE EW)

SERVES 2

When you ask people what their favorite Thai food is, Pad Thai is the most common answer. *Excuse me?* Are we gonna pretend that Pad See Ew doesn't exist? She is very gorgeous to meeee!

Whenever I order Thai food, whether at a restaurant or on a delivery app, pad see ew will always be on the table—no questions asked. There are so many things to love about it. Those amazing wide noodles, the tender beef that falls apart in your mouth, the crunchy broccolini. The eggs are alright. Eggs just taste like eggs.

One of my favorite Thai restaurants, responsible for my love of Pad See Ew, is none other than Sapp Coffee Shop in Thai Town, Los Angeles. I just felt like giving them a shout-out because the staff is amazing and they have the best food. Did I mention the restaurant is also woman-owned and run?

FOR THE MEAT AND MARINADE

8 ounces flank steak, thinly sliced against the grain

1 tablespoon soy sauce

1 teaspoon cornstarch

½ teaspoon avocado oil

½ teaspoon sugar

FOR THE SAUCE

1½ tablespoons oyster sauce

2 teaspoons dark soy sauce

1 teaspoon soy sauce

2 teaspoons sugar

1 teaspoon rice vinegar

1. Combine the meat and all of the marinade ingredients in a medium bowl. Mix well and allow to marinate at room temperature for 30 minutes.

2. Meanwhile, for the sauce, combine all the sauce ingredients in a small bowl.

3. For the stir-fry: Separate the noodles and set them aside on a plate. Heat 1 tablespoon of the avocado oil in a large pan or wok over high heat. Add the meat, using a spatula to spread the pieces evenly. Let the meat brown for about 1 minute, then stir-fry for an additional minute. Transfer to a plate and set aside.

4. Add the remaining 1 tablespoon avocado oil to the hot pan, then add the broccoli stems and the garlic. Stir-fry until the garlic is fragrant, about 30 seconds. Add the rice noodles and stir-fry until warmed through, about 1 minute. Drizzle the sauce over the noodles and mix well so that they are evenly incorporated. Return the meat to the pan, along with the leafy part of the Chinese broccoli, and toss together.

FOR THE STIR-FRY

8 ounces fresh wide rice noodles

2 tablespoons avocado oil

4 ounces Chinese broccoli, cut into 1-inch pieces, stems and leaves separated

4 garlic cloves, minced

2 large eggs

FOR FINISHING

Pinch of MSG

¼ teaspoon freshly ground black pepper

5. Push all of the ingredients to one side and crack the eggs directly into the pan. Allow the eggs to cook through for about 30 seconds, then scramble and mix with the other ingredients.

6. Season with a pinch of MSG and the pepper. Remove from heat and transfer to a serving bowl. Enjoy!

To make beautiful curly scallions, slice very thinly on a diagonal. Then, place in ice-cold water and refrigerate until they're ready to be used.

BEEF UDON (NIKU UDON)

SERVES 2

FOR THE DASHI

4 cups water

1 tablespoon Hondashi powder

2½ tablespoons soy sauce

1 tablespoon mirin

FOR THE BEEF

8 ounces thinly sliced rib eye, or any other beef (see sidebar)

1 tablespoon soy sauce

1 tablespoon sake

2 teaspoons mirin

2 teaspoons sugar

½ yellow onion, sliced (about ½ cup)

2 scallions, sliced, white and green parts separated

FOR FINISHING

12 ounces frozen udon noodles (see Notes)

4 thin slices narutomaki (see Notes; optional)

Shichimi togarashi (optional)

Working on this recipe book, I got sick of eating a lot of stuff. I think since I was constantly cooking, I got overstimulated very easily. I touched a lot of different ingredients, smelled the food cooking, and when it got to actually eating the food, I was tapped out. Especially fried food. Oh my god, I don't think I'm going to touch fried food for months (except fried chicken, my true love, see page 36).

But one meal I never got tired of eating was beef udon, or niku udon. This noodle dish is just so simple at its core: seasoned dashi broth with udon noodles and thinly sliced beef mixed with onions—that's it. Dashi is a Japanese stock that is used as the base of many Japanese dishes. It's typically made with kombu (a type of seaweed) and bonito flakes, and has a rich, umami taste.

This recipe is really beginner, as we use Hondashi (dashi powder) to make our broth, instead of the traditional kombu and bonito flakes. (But if desired, you can make the dashi from scratch using the recipe from our miso soup on page 16.) No fancy cuts of beef, no deep-frying anything—this is a simple meal that is as reliable as a Honda Civic. Also! If you're looking to pair something with this meal, my favorite partner is shrimp tempura (I buy them frozen and just air fry them).

1. For the dashi, bring the water to a simmer in a medium pot over medium-high heat. Add the Hondashi powder, soy sauce, and mirin. Mix well and turn off the heat. Set aside while you prepare the beef and noodles.

2. For the beef, in a medium pan, combine the beef, soy sauce, sake, mirin, sugar, onion, and sliced scallion whites (save the green parts for garnish). Add 1 cup of the dashi, mix

recipe continues

together well, and bring to a simmer over medium-low heat. Simmer until the beef and onions are tender, about 12 minutes.

3. While the beef is simmering, cook the noodles according to the package instructions. (If the package doesn't include a time, boil the noodles in salted water for about 8 minutes, until al dente.) Drain and divide between two bowls.

4. Bring the dashi back to a simmer. Pour over the noodles, dividing evenly between the two bowls. Then, divide the meat, onion, and cooking liquid evenly between the two bowls.

5. Top with narutomaki, sliced scallion greens, and togarashi if desired.

NOTES: *Udon is really easy to find in Asian grocery stores. They're typically located in the frozen section of the store.*

Narutomaki is a fish cake found in most Asian grocery stores, in the refrigerator/freezer section alongside the tofu. Its shape is a long stick, and can be recognized by its pink swirl.

SHABU MEAT

Thinly sliced beef is available at most Asian grocery stores. It can be found fresh, in the meat section, or frozen in plastic containers within the same area. What you'll be looking for is meat labeled *shabu meat*. The meat is thinly sliced and sometimes curled up into rolls. If not readily available, you can use your favorite cut of meat. Simply put it in the freezer for about 30 minutes to firm up the meat, then use your sharpest knife to slice against the grain as thinly as you can.

KOREAN SOYBEAN PASTE SOUP (DOENJANG–JJIGAE)

SERVES 1

I'm sure you've seen this soup in your favorite Korean drama, when the oppa is feeding it to his love interest. Too bad you'll never experience that in your lifetime. It's okay, Oppar Newt will teach you how to make it so you can feed yourself. The soup is spicy, comforting, and filled with nutritious vegetables. We even spruce things up by adding enoki mushrooms, which provide a fun chewy texture. It's a no-brainer why this soup is so popular and my default soup when ordering from any Korean BBQ joint.

2½ cups water

1½ teaspoons anchovy stock powder

2 tablespoons doenjang (Korean soybean paste)

2 teaspoons gochugaru (Korean pepper flakes)

½ zucchini, quartered and sliced

½ small yellow onion, cut into ½-inch pieces

2 garlic cloves, minced

5 ounces beef, thinly sliced (see Shabu Meat sidebar, page 96)

4 ounces medium-firm tofu, cut into small rectangles

2 ounces enoki mushrooms, bottom part of stems cut off

FOR FINISHING

½ serrano chile, sliced

1 scallion, green part only, sliced

1. Place the water in a Korean clay pot (dolsot) or a small, heavy pot and bring to a simmer over medium heat. Add the anchovy powder, soybean paste, and gochugaru. Mix well, until the paste dissolves in the water, and bring back to a simmer.

2. Add the zucchini, onion, and garlic to the pot and bring back to a simmer over medium-high heat. Cover and reduce the heat so that the stew remains at a simmer. Cook until the vegetables have softened, about 4 minutes.

3. Uncover and stir in the beef, tofu, and mushrooms. Bring back to a simmer and cook for another 2 minutes, until the beef is cooked through and the mushrooms have softened. Remove from the heat.

4. Top with serrano chiles and scallion greens. Serve alongside a bowl of white rice. Enjoy!

NOTE: *The main star of this dish is doenjang, the Korean fermented soybean paste. This paste lasts forever in the fridge, which is why I always have it on hand and use it whenever I want a flavor boost in my soups. Doenjang can be found at Korean grocery stores or online.*

PERUVIAN BEEF STIR-FRY (LOMO SALTADO)

SERVES 2 TO 3

It is a regular Monday when I walk into Rikas Peruvian Cuisine in L.A., ready to order lunch. To the cashier, I say, "Can I get the lomo saltado, please?" The middle-aged cashier rings me up and collects my payment. To my shock, she says, "You smell so good!" I blush and thank her for the compliment. That is a true story and this lomo saltado recipe is dedicated to that cashier.

Lomo saltado is a Peruvian stir-fry with steak, tomatoes, onions, and french fries (plus other ingredients). Yes, you heard that right. When I first learned about this dish, I thought it was so bizarre. I couldn't believe I was about to eat a stir-fry containing french fries (a carb), with a side of rice. Isn't that a double carb violation? Or a win-win situation?

12 ounces sirloin steak, cut against the grain into thin slices

1 teaspoon kosher salt

1 teaspoon ground cumin

FOR THE SAUCE

2 tablespoons oyster sauce

2 tablespoons soy sauce

2 tablespoons aji amarillo paste (see Note)

1 tablespoon white vinegar

FOR THE STIR-FRY

3 tablespoons avocado oil

2 Roma tomatoes, quartered, cored, seeded, and sliced

½ red onion, sliced

2 scallions, cut into 2-inch pieces

4 garlic cloves, minced

6 ounces cooked french fries

3 tablespoons chopped fresh cilantro

1 teaspoon freshly ground black pepper

1. Place the sliced steak in a medium mixing bowl and season with the salt and cumin. Mix well and leave to marinate at room temperature for 30 minutes.

2. For the sauce, mix all the sauce ingredients in a small bowl and set aside.

3. For the stir-fry, heat a wok or frying pan over high heat until the pan begins to smoke a little. Add 2 tablespoons of the avocado oil and the beef. Cook, stirring occasionally, until all of the meat is browned, about 3 minutes. Remove to a plate or bowl and set aside.

4. Heat the remaining 1 tablespoon oil in the same wok and add the tomatoes, onion, and scallions. Cook until the onion is slightly charred on the outside, 1½ to 2 minutes. Add the garlic and cook until fragrant, about 30 seconds. Return the beef to the pan, stir-fry for an additional minute, and stir in the sauce. Add the french fries, cilantro, and black pepper, mix one last time, then remove from the heat and serve.

NOTE: *Aji amarillo paste is a Peruvian paste made with Peru's hot yellow chiles. You can find it on Amazon and at many Hispanic markets.*

VIETNAMESE SHAKING BEEF (BÒ LÚC LẮC)

SERVES 2

FOR THE BÒ LÚC LẮC SAUCE

2 tablespoons condensed milk

2 tablespoons Maggi seasoning

1 tablespoon BBQ sauce

1 tablespoon oyster sauce

1 tablespoon hoisin sauce

1 tablespoon dark sesame oil

FOR THE BÒ LÚC LẮC

2 tablespoons avocado oil

8 ounces filet mignon, cut into 1-inch cubes

1 teaspoon kosher salt

½ medium green bell pepper, cut into 1-inch squares

½ medium red bell pepper, cut into 1-inch squares

⅓ medium yellow onion, cut into 1-inch squares

1 large jalapeño chile, sliced

2 plump garlic cloves, minced

2 tablespoons salted butter

Freshly cracked black pepper, for garnish

Fresh cilantro sprigs, for garnish

Vietnamese shaking beef was the number-one bestselling dish at the restaurant I worked at when I was a teenager. I can't think of bò lúc lắc without remembering the wokmaster at my work, Chú Lam.

Standing at five feet two, Lam would chef up dozens of orders of these tender meat cubes per day. He was probably the hardest worker we had, because he worked the longest hours, the most days, and was pretty much everyone's emotional punching bag. What was admirable was how he always had a smile on his face, and how caring he was for the workers. He would make sure that we were well fed, always offering a giant portion of these steak cubes with rice.

This bò lúc lắc is a re-creation of Lam's dish. What sets the recipe apart from other versions is the addition of condensed milk. It might sound weird at first, but condensed milk actually does a great job of sweetening a sauce and caramelizes well on meat. I think once you try this bò lúc lắc, you'll understand why it sold so well at the restaurant.

Have all of the ingredients prepped and within reach before you begin. Once the cooking starts you will be moving pretty quickly!

1. For the sauce (see Note): In a small bowl, whisk together all of the sauce ingredients. Set aside.

2. Heat a wok over high heat. Add the avocado oil, toss in the cubed beef, and season with the salt. Brown the meat on all sides, 3 to 4 minutes (see Free Game).

3. Toss in the green and red peppers, onion, and jalapeño. Stir-fry until slightly charred, 1 to 2 minutes. Toss in the garlic and sauté for 30 seconds, until fragrant. Add the sauce, stir well, and stir-fry for up to 1 minute, until the sauce coats the

meat and caramelizes. Add the butter and allow it to melt. Give everything a nice toss and remove from the heat.

4. Garnish with freshly cracked black pepper and cilantro sprigs and serve with rice, such as steamed jasmine rice.

NOTE: *You will only need about half the sauce here. So, you can make the recipe two times! What I like to do is to cover the sauce and refrigerate for future use. It can last up to 1 week in the fridge.*

FREE GAME

When browning meat, avoid moving it too much, as that interferes with the browning process.

There are two reasons I cook. To make TikTok videos, or to impress others. I actually never cook for myself unless it's instant ramen noodles, which is my other obsession besides fried chicken. Most of the time, I just order delivery because I hate doing dishes, and eating out of a delivery box while playing computer games is a vibe.

But to impress people, you can't just cook *anything*.

Imagine going to a date's house and they cook you Spam, eggs, and rice. Although it's a damn good meal and I'd be grateful they even took the time to make me something in the first place, it's also what I learned to cook myself when I was eight years old. Baby, we have to raise our standards. It's 2024.

This chapter contains recipes that are specifically for those who want to leave a lasting impression. Whether it be for your date, girlfriend/boyfriend, or your homies visiting from out of town—it doesn't matter. These recipes are so good that they'll have your guest wanting to lean in and give you a smoochie on the cheek. I will say, they are "heavier" recipes, as they contain pasta, steak, and short ribs. Which means you might have to unbutton your pants after eating so that you can breathe (we've all been there).

KISS THE CHEF

PASTA POMODORO WITH MEATBALLS

SERVES ABOUT 4

If you told the young version of me that in the future I'd be coming out with a cookbook that contained a red sauce spaghetti recipe, I would've literally projectile vomited. As a kid I hated tomatoes. I despised ketchup even more (still do). However, maturing means retrying foods and realizing they aren't so bad after all. I think one of the main reasons I disliked spaghetti is because it was served so often for lunch at school. Kids aren't the cleanest creatures, so I remember seeing spaghetti being spilled on the lunch tables and (sometimes) floor, and the smell of that thick, meaty, tomatoey sauce traumatized me.

Pasta pomodoro is spaghetti's hotter, Chad-like cousin. The difference between the two sauces mostly lies in the fact that pomodoro doesn't contain minced meat in the sauce itself, and is much more smooth. I chose to adjust the traditional pomodoro recipe by including really flavorful and tender meatballs, because I felt like it made the entire dish feel more complete and hearty. While developing this recipe, I had to make and taste the sauce so many times, but I was happy to do so because I wanted it to be perfect. The end result was a sauce that I felt I (a previous tomato hater) could really appreciate, tasting each and every ingredient. I know I sound like a cringe wine sommelier trying to convince you to savor every note of grape that was squished and aged into a wine, but it's true. I've come to really like tomatoes, and I think if you like tomatoes too, you'll really love this dish.

FOR THE MEATBALLS

8 ounces 80 percent lean ground beef

8 ounces ground pork

½ small yellow onion, grated (use the other half for the sauce)

12 cloves Garlic Confit (page 191), minced, or 1 tablespoon garlic powder

½ cup panko breadcrumbs

⅓ cup freshly grated Parmesan

1. For the meatballs: In a mixing bowl, combine all of the meatball ingredients except the olive oil and mix gently with your hands. Be careful not to overmix, as it'll yield a dense meatball. Excessive pressure makes the meatballs too dense. We want a meatball that is nice and moist, not hard and dry. My favorite technique for mixing without squishing the meat is to use a claw grip. Shape your mixing hand into a claw, as if you're some type of bird, and mix.

2. Line a baking sheet with parchment. Using a 1½-inch cookie scoop or your hands, shape the mixture into meatballs and place them on the parchment (as soon as they take on their shape, set them down). The parchment paper prevents

recipe continues

1 large egg

3 tablespoons whole milk

2 tablespoons chopped fresh parsley

1 teaspoon kosher salt

1 teaspoon Italian seasoning

½ teaspoon red pepper flakes, plus more if desired

½ teaspoon freshly cracked black pepper

2 tablespoons olive oil (for browning)

FOR THE POMODORO SAUCE

2 tablespoons olive oil

½ yellow onion, minced

One 28-ounce can whole San Marzano tomatoes

6 garlic cloves, peeled and smashed

1 tablespoon sugar

1 teaspoon dried oregano

1 teaspoon kosher salt

½ teaspoon freshly cracked black pepper

12 fresh basil leaves, roughly torn into pieces

FOR THE PASTA

1 pound spaghetti

Freshly grated Parmesan, for serving

Fresh basil leaves, for serving

the meatballs from sticking. Cover with plastic and refrigerate for 1 hour, or up to 24 hours. This allows the meatballs to season, as well as hold their shape better when frying.

3. When ready to cook, heat the olive oil a heavy-bottomed pot over medium heat. In two batches, add the meatballs and cook, moving them around in the pan to brown evenly on all sides. It should take 3 to 4 minutes per batch. Remove from the heat and set aside on a plate. Scrape away all of the burnt bits of meat and discard any fat remaining in the pan.

4. To make the sauce, add the olive oil to the pan and reduce the heat to medium-low. Add the minced onion and sauté until softened, about 5 minutes. Add the whole tomatoes with their liquid, garlic, sugar, oregano, salt, pepper, and basil. Mix together well, bring to a simmer, and cook for 10 minutes, until the tomatoes have broken down slightly and the liquid has reduced.

5. Transfer the sauce to a blender and blend until smooth, about 30 seconds. Return to the pot and bring back to a simmer over low heat. Add the meatballs and cover partially. Simmer for another 30 minutes, stirring occasionally to move the meatballs around (but not too much), until the meatballs are fully cooked.

6. While the sauce and meatballs are simmering, bring a large pot of salted water to a boil and cook the spaghetti per the package instructions. Drain.

7. To serve, toss each serving of pasta with about ½ cup of sauce in a bowl and place on a serving plate or a wide bowl. Top each bowl with more sauce if desired and five or six meatballs. Garnish with grated Parmesan and fresh basil leaves and serve.

FREE GAME

Although it's common practice to use the "fond," or browned bits left after cooking meat, I find with this sauce that the oil and bits at the bottom of the pan typically turn black. Browned bits = flavor, but blackened bits = bitter and will mess up the sauce.

SPICY VODKA PASTA

SERVES 3 TO 4

8 ounces fusilli or rigatoni

Kosher salt

2 tablespoons olive oil

¼ medium yellow onion, chopped

3 garlic cloves, minced

4 tablespoons tomato paste

2 tablespoons vodka (omit if you don't drink alcohol)

4 tablespoons unsalted butter

1 tablespoon Calabrian chili paste (see sidebar, page 67)

¼ teaspoon sugar

¾ cup heavy cream

½ to 2 teaspoons red pepper flakes, depending on spice tolerance

Freshly grated Parmesan, for serving

Fresh basil leaves, whole or chiffonade (thinly sliced into strips), for serving

Spicy vodka pasta is one of those dishes that had everyone on social media in a *choke hold* during quarantine. It's up there with the founding fathers of quarantine food/drink creations—dalgona coffee, baked feta pasta, cloud bread. You just had to be there to experience it. However, I learned about it in a different way.

Carbone introduced me to spicy vodka pasta. The famous New York restaurant is known as a gathering spot for celebrities, all coming together for one thing—their spicy rigatoni. Having tried it myself (in their much less cool Las Vegas restaurant because I've never been able to get a table at the one in New York), I completely understand the hype.

This dish is the definition of comfort food. As you take a bite, you're greeted with a fantastic creamy tomato sauce. But not before the kick of spice introduces itself, thanks to the Calabrian chili paste. As the pasta travels down to your stomach, your grandmother appears and gives you a nice, warm hug (my grandma has never hugged me, btw, I'm just using my imagination). All is right in the world. Whenever I find myself in a lower vibrational mood, this is the one dish that I gravitate towards. No meat, no fancy ingredients, just a big bowl of comforting pasta.

recipe continues

1. Cook the pasta in a large pot of boiling salted water per the package instructions. Drain, reserving 1 cup of the pasta water and set aside. (Typically, I make the pasta sauce and cook the pasta at the same time. In this recipe, I suggest cooking the pasta first to make it as fail proof as possible. If you're confident, you can totally cook the pasta and sauce at the same time.)

2. Heat the olive oil in a large skillet over medium heat. Add the onion and ½ teaspoon salt and cook until the onion softens, 2 to 3 minutes. Add the garlic and cook until fragrant, about 30 seconds. Stir in the tomato paste and cook, stirring, until it has darkened in color, about 4 minutes. (Allowing the tomato paste to caramelize will ensure a deep, rich flavor.)

3. Add the vodka and, using a wooden spoon, stir and scrape any browned bits from the bottom of the pan to deglaze. Let the alcohol cook off for about 30 seconds, then stir in the butter, chili paste, and sugar. Stir until the butter has melted.

4. Transfer the sauce to a blender, add the cream and ¾ cup of the reserved pasta water, and blend until smooth, 1 to 2 minutes. Taste the sauce for salt. If you find that it's under-salted, add a pinch of salt at a time, to your liking.

5. Return your skillet to low heat (we're only doing this to warm up the pasta), add the pasta and the sauce, along with the red pepper flakes, and mix well.

6. Serve with a generous amount of grated Parmesan, more red pepper flakes (if desired), and fresh basil. Enjoy!

FREE GAME

What's the point of adding pasta water and butter to a sauce? The answer can be summed up in one word: emulsification. Have you ever wondered why the pasta at your local restaurant tastes better than the pasta that you make at home? It's because they're vigorously mixing your pasta in a sauce containing starchy, salty pasta water and lots of butter. So, save some of your pasta water when you cook pasta, because your sauce needs the starch and salt.

SPICY SAUSAGE PASTA

SERVES 2 GENEROUSLY

Kosher salt

8 ounces dried cavatelli pasta

2 tablespoons olive oil

1 spicy sausage (about 4 ounces), removed from the casing and broken into pea-size pieces

2 garlic cloves, peeled and smashed

2 teaspoons Italian seasoning

2 tablespoons dry white wine, like chardonnay

½ cup heavy cream

¼ cup freshly grated Parmesan

Freshly ground pepper, to taste

Shaved black truffle, for serving (optional; see sidebar)

One of the first "upscale" restaurants I went to when I first moved to Los Angeles was Bestia. I know it's upscale because on Yelp it has three dollar signs ($) next to its name. To date, I've paid the restaurant a visit a couple times, and will keep coming back for three dishes—the grilled branzino, the roasted bone marrow pasta, and pasta alla norcina.

A creamy, spicy Italian pasta dish with sausage, pasta alla norcina is one of the most delectable items on Bestia's menu. The star of the show is actually the pasta shape—cavatelli. Finding cavatelli might require you to get into contact with your local pasta dealer, but the result is well worth it. This pasta shape is chewy, which is the perfect texture for our creamy, umami wine sauce. For special occasions, we shave a bit of black truffle right on top to make this dish even more delicious. No seriously, only do this on special occasions because black truffles are expensive, about eighty dollars per gram (which, fun fact, is on par with the price of cocaine). If you're making this casually, ditch the truffle and replace cavatelli with rigatoni. :)

Disclaimer: I'm not talking from personal experience—I literally just googled the price of the drug out of pure curiosity. Don't do drugs! They're illegal and bad for you.

FREE GAME

Sauce too runny = Add more grated Parmesan cheese.
Sauce too thick = Add more pasta water.

1. Bring a large pot of water to a boil and salt generously. Add the pasta and cook for 12 to 15 minutes, until cooked al dente.

2. Meanwhile, heat a skillet over medium-high heat and add the olive oil. Add the sausage, garlic, and Italian seasoning and cook for 3 to 4 minutes, until the meat is nicely browned. Add the white wine and stir with a rubber spatula or wooden spoon, scraping up all of the good bits from the bottom of the pan to deglaze. Cook, stirring, until all of the wine has evaporated, about 1 minute. Remove and discard the garlic cloves. Stir in the cream, bring to a simmer, and cook, stirring often, until the sauce has reduced and the sausage is cooked through, 2 to 3 minutes.

3. Drain the pasta, making sure to reserve some of the cooking water so you can adjust the consistency of the sauce. Add the pasta to the sauce and mix well. Remove from the heat and stir in the Parmesan. One tablespoon at a time, add enough pasta cooking water to give the sauce a creamy consistency, usually 3 to 4 tablespoons. Taste and adjust salt. Transfer to plates, top with freshly ground pepper and shaved truffle (if you like), and serve.

TRUFFLES

Truffles are edible fungi that are mostly sourced from European countries like Italy, France, and Spain, though they grow elsewhere. Truffle hunters use animals with a heightened sense of smell—like dogs and pigs—to find them. I know, the thought of a dog sniffing for truffles is freaking cute. They're expensive because truffles only grow under certain conditions and during certain parts of the year, and once they're harvested, they have a very short shelf life, about 10 days. I get fresh truffles from a company called Urbani, which supplies many New York restaurants. Urbani has an online site that ships to your doorstep in a few days, and they often have sales throughout the year as well. Alternatively, you can purchase truffles at an Eataly, if you happen to live near one.

CHICKEN PARM

SERVES 2

1 (6- to 8-ounce) boneless skinless chicken breast

1 teaspoon kosher salt, or to taste

1 teaspoon freshly cracked black pepper, or to taste

1 teaspoon garlic powder, or to taste

¼ cup all-purpose flour

1 large egg, beaten

1 cup Italian breadcrumbs

¼ cup olive oil

1 cup marinara sauce

4 ounces (about 1 cup) shredded mozzarella

2 tablespoons freshly grated Parmesan

1 tablespoon chopped fresh Italian parsley, for garnish

The first time I made chicken Parmesan, it looked like I dropped a fried chicken cutlet on freshly cut grass trimmings—but people on Twitter still hyped me up. I love it. This chicken Parm recipe is actually inspired by one of my favorite food personalities, Matty Matheson. He has a restaurant called Rizzo's House of Parm that serves a chicken Parm that is so insanely loaded with cheese that it could be mistaken for pizza. Seeing as I'm about 2,000 miles away from the restaurant, I decided to have a quirky DIY moment at home instead.

A chicken breast is a boring piece of meat, unless it's, ummm, I don't know . . . sliced thinly and seasoned. Quickly breaded with flour, egg, and Italian breadcrumbs. Tossed into hot oil to fry until crisp. Lathered with marinara sauce, topped with cheese, and baked until it's, well . . . essentially a pizza with chicken for crust. This chicken Parm dish is delicious to say the least, and guaranteed to leave a lasting impression on anyone.

1. Slice the chicken breast in half horizontally by placing one hand on top of the breast and using the other to slice through the middle.

2. One at a time, place the chicken cutlets in a gallon-size ziplock bag and pound with a hammer or meat tenderizer until about ½ inch thick. Don't pound too hard! You don't want to tear the chicken. Season both sides with salt, pepper, and garlic powder.

3. Prepare the breading station by setting out three soup plates, one with the flour, another with the beaten egg, and the third with the breadcrumbs.

recipe continues

4. Heat the olive oil in a wide pan over medium heat. While the oil heats, bread the chicken cutlets by dipping one first in the flour, then the egg, and finally the Italian breadcrumbs. I like to press on the breadcrumbs at the end, just to ensure I have a nice crust! Repeat with the remaining cutlet.

5. When the oil is hot, carefully lay the breaded cutlets in the pan. Cook until the internal temperature reads 165°F or higher, about 2½ minutes, turning halfway through and using a spoon to baste any uneven spots with the hot olive oil.

6. Transfer the cutlets to a paper towel–lined plate or a wire rack set in a baking sheet. Then, transfer to an oven-safe plate or a large baking sheet.

7. Preheat the broiler. Spoon the marinara sauce over the chicken and top with the mozzarella and Parmesan. I like to go overboard with the cheeses because I love the way the cheese browns under the broiler, like a delicious, crispy snack.

8. Place under the preheated broiler on the top rack and broil until the cheese is nicely browned, 3 to 4 minutes. Remove from the oven, top with parsley, and enjoy!

KOREAN SHORT RIBS (GALBI)

SERVES 5

FOR THE MEAT AND MARINADE

2½ pounds thin-cut beef short ribs, thawed if frozen (see Note)

½ yellow onion, chopped

½ Korean pear, peeled, cored, and roughly chopped

3 scallions, chopped

4 to 5 garlic cloves, peeled, or more to taste

¾ cup packed brown sugar

½ cup pineapple juice

½ cup regular soy sauce

3 tablespoons dark soy sauce

¼ cup mirin

3 tablespoons sesame oil

2 tablespoons white sesame seeds

½ teaspoon freshly ground black pepper

¼ teaspoon MSG

FOR SEARING THE SHORT RIBS AND FINISHING

About 4 tablespoons avocado oil, as needed

Sesame seeds, to taste

Sliced scallions, to taste

At my childhood family barbecues, I could guarantee a few things—Heineken, horrible karaoke, and Korean short ribs. Looking back, it's actually kind of funny because none of us are Korean, and I literally did not know one single Korean person until I moved to Los Angeles. But that's beside the point.

Korean short ribs, or galbi, is a staple food in my life. Whether it's from when I was a kid or now, my love for it is like a fire that cannot be extinguished. There's something about the sweet marinade that is so delicious when the ribs are grilled over an open flame. When I'm cooking my own at Korean BBQ spots, I always cook it extra burnt, because that smoky flavor is so addictive. And yes, I eat every part of it, including the cartilage. Sometimes when I'm extra hungry I even suck the bone to get more of the marinade out (but only when I'm desperate). If you have access to an Asian grocery store, like H Mart, you can buy prepackaged marinade and season your short ribs that way. This recipe is specifically for those who really want to make and adjust the marinade on their own, or live in areas that don't have Asian grocery stores (you should move to a new neighborhood). Either way, everyone deserves to experience the deliciousness of galbi. It will change lives.

recipe continues

1. Place the short ribs in a large bowl and cover with water until completely submerged. Using your hands, rub the meat and bones, removing any impurities or bone shavings from the cutting process. Drain and replace the water. Allow the beef to soak at room temperature for 30 minutes.

2. Meanwhile, for the marinade: Combine all of the marinade ingredients in a blender and blend on high until smooth, about 45 seconds.

3. Drain the meat and transfer to a gallon-size ziplock bag. Add the marinade and seal the bag. Refrigerate for 12 to 24 hours.

4. Heat 1 tablespoon of the avocado oil in a large nonstick pan over medium-high heat. Remove the short ribs from the ziplock bag, letting as much marinade as possible drip off. In batches, add the short ribs to the hot oil and cook until slightly charred and cooked through, about 2 minutes on each side. Transfer to a serving plate. Repeat until all of the short ribs are seared, adding more oil to the pan in between batches if necessary. If the marinade becomes burnt in the pan, simply wipe with a paper towel.

5. Top the short ribs with sesame seeds and scallions. Enjoy!

NOTE: *To make Korean short ribs, we use a specific cut of beef short rib that can be referred to as thin cut, flanken, or cross-cut. The ribs are cut lengthwise, making it easier to prepare and eat! They're readily available at most grocery stores, from Asian or Mexican specialty supermarkets to Whole Foods.*

FREE GAME

We soak the meat for 30 minutes to remove "blood" from the meat, giving us a cleaner "canvas" to soak up the delicious marinade.

RED WINE BRAISED SHORT RIBS

SERVES 4 TO 6

3 tablespoons avocado oil

3 pounds bone-in short ribs

Kosher salt

1 medium yellow onion, coarsely chopped

3 medium carrots, coarsely sliced

2 stalks celery, coarsely sliced

3 tablespoons tomato paste

½ cup red wine

2 heads garlic, cut in half crosswise

3 sprigs fresh rosemary

8 sprigs fresh thyme

1 bay leaf

3 cups beef stock, plus more as needed

1 teaspoon whole black peppercorns

1 tablespoon unsalted butter

Chopped fresh parsley and/or chives, for garnish

Before I started cooking, there were just two things that really scared me. Insanely buff meatheads at the gym who wear stringer tank tops that just barely cover their milkers, and braising short ribs. For whatever reason, I subconsciously decided that making short ribs was a hard task. I mean, how can making meat that falls off the bone possibly be easy? Making such delicate meat can only be the result of hard work and skillful cooking. I was wrong.

Braising is cooking something in fat and liquid over a long period of time to break apart its connective tissue and turn the tough piece of meat into a tender bite of deliciousness. This recipe is genuinely one of my favorites because its effort-to-reward ratio is just about unmatched. The active cooking time is less than 30 minutes, and then you kind of just let it chill in a meat sauna for 3 hours to finish cooking. I usually take this time to play video games, either Valorant or TFT. After I lose all my games, I still feel okay inside, because I'll be comforted by a plate of fall-apart short ribs that will love me no matter what.

1. Preheat the oven to 275°F.

2. Heat the oil over medium-high heat in a heavy pot, such as a Dutch oven. Dry the short ribs with a paper towel and season generously with salt. In two batches, add to the pan and sear on all sides for about 1 minute per side, until the outsides develop a nice, deep brown crust. Each batch should take about 5 minutes. Transfer the meat to a plate.

3. Reduce the heat to medium-low and add the onion, carrots, and celery to the pot. Season with ½ teaspoon salt and cook until the vegetables have softened and developed

recipe continues

some color, about 8 minutes. Add the tomato paste and continue to cook, stirring often, for about 4 minutes, until the tomato paste deepens in color. Add the red wine to deglaze the pan. Bring to a simmer while you scrape the browned bits from the bottom and sides of the pan with a rubber spatula or wooden spoon. Allow to simmer for at least 1 minute so that all of the alcohol evaporates.

4. Return the short ribs to the pot, along with the halved heads of garlic, the rosemary, thyme, bay leaf, and peppercorns. Add the beef stock (it should cover the meat) and bring to a simmer. Skim off all the foam and impurities from the surface.

5. Cover with a piece of parchment, or partially cover with a lid, and transfer to the preheated oven. Braise for 3 hours, or until the short ribs are fork-tender.

6. Carefully transfer the short ribs to a bowl and cover to keep warm. Strain the broth into a saucepan and discard the vegetables and herbs. Bring the broth to a boil over medium-high heat and reduce until it thickens slightly. Whisk or stir in the cold butter and continue to boil until the sauce reaches your desired consistency, 14 to 16 minutes for a nice, thick sauce. Taste and adjust salt.

7. Serve the short ribs over mashed potatoes, topped with plenty of sauce and garnished with chives or parsley.

FREE GAME

The vegetables can be roughly cut, as they'll be discarded later on. Just make sure they're cut around the same size so they cook evenly!

The term for covering with a piece of parchment instead of a lid is *cartouche.*

STEAK WITH CHIMICHURRI SAUCE

SERVES 2

FOR THE CHIMICHURRI

3 tablespoons olive oil

1 tablespoon red wine vinegar

3 tablespoons finely minced fresh parsley

3 garlic cloves, finely minced

½ Fresno chile pepper, seeded and finely minced

1 teaspoon dried oregano

¼ teaspoon kosher salt

¼ teaspoon freshly ground black pepper

FOR THE STEAK

One 1-pound rib eye or New York strip steak, about 1 inch thick

1½ tablespoons avocado oil

Kosher salt

2 tablespoons unsalted butter

3 garlic cloves, peeled and lightly smashed

2 sprigs fresh thyme

1 sprig fresh rosemary

Steak should always be served medium to medium-rare. Not cremated and well-done (the cow didn't die for this), and not rare to the point where it's mooing either. I will die on this hill.

In today's age, we're exposed to so many different methods of cooking steak. Reverse sear, sous vide, or grilled over an open flame: although these methods can yield great results, they take so much time and commitment. In this recipe, we're keeping things simple by going back to the good ol' pan. Steak doesn't have to be difficult. All it takes is a few minutes on each side on high heat to develop a beautiful and delicious crust. Then, we baste it in butter, garlic, and herbs to layer on more flavor!

I love steak with chimichurri sauce, the Argentinean sauce of garlic, chiles, herbs, vinegar, and olive oil. Paired with steak, it provides a Super-Mario-Kart-mushroom boost in flavor. The best way to describe it is herbaceous and garlicky—everything I want and more.

recipe continues

1. Combine all the chimichurri ingredients in a bowl and mix well. Set aside.

2. When ready to cook, pat all sides of the steak dry with a paper towel. Place a wire rack in a small baking sheet.

3. Heat a heavy pan, such as cast-iron or carbon-steel, over medium-high heat until slightly smoking. Add the avocado oil and heat it until shimmering. Generously season the steak on all sides with salt, then lay in the pan. Using tongs, press down on the steak to ensure it makes full contact with the pan. Cook for a total of 6 minutes and 30 seconds, flipping every 2 minutes (1 minute and 15 seconds on each side at the end). Remove the steak from the pan and rest it on the rack in the baking sheet.

4. Reduce the heat to low, then add the butter to the pan, along with the garlic, thyme, and rosemary. Once the butter has melted and become bubbly, return the steak to the pan. Cook, using a spoon to baste the steak with the butter for 30 seconds on each side, until it reaches an internal temperature of 130°F for medium-rare, or 140°F for medium. (You can check the temperature of the steak by inserting a meat thermometer right into the middle.)

5. Transfer the steak to the wire rack in the baking sheet and let rest for at least 5 minutes. Transfer to a cutting board and slice against the grain. Serve the chimichurri sauce on the side.

FREE GAME

The reason we only season our steak with salt is because most seasoning will burn during the searing process. A good steak only needs salt. For those who want more flavor, don't worry! We'll be getting flavor from the chimichurri. And if you want even more, try the delicious Cajun Butter (page 186) that I like to blowtorch right on top of the steak.

OXTAIL RAGU

SERVES 5

Oxtail used to be cheap. In the past, it was considered "scrap meat," undesirable to the majority of people and to be consumed by the poor because, well, nobody wanted it. So, you might be asking yourself, "Why does it cost so much today, and why is it used by so many upscale restaurants?" Well, for starters, an ox has only one tail, which isn't that big compared to the rest of its body, which means there's not much of it. Not to mention that it gained a lot of popularity once people found out how tender its meat can be when cooked properly. We should've gatekept this from the rich, smh.

Oxtail ragu has to be one of my favorite pasta dishes because it's absolutely so, so tender. The oxtail pieces are browned then braised in a tomato sauce for 4 hours, then later combined with my favorite pasta shape—pappardelle. There's something special about pappardelle's thickness that does such a great job of carrying this meat sauce into one's mouth. It's incredible. This braised dish is a bit different from my other ones in the use of Parmesan cheese rind. Many people discard the rind because they think it's hard and inedible, but that's not true. Throwing a cheese rind into a braise adds a lot of umami—just remember to give it a good wash first.

Sidebar: I know that as cooks, we should really appreciate and understand where foods come from, but for a while I didn't actually make the connection that oxtail was the tail of an ox (but sliced up). Holy shit. It first clicked in my head when I saw a TikTok video of a guy chopping up the tail of some mysterious creature that turned out to be an ox.

2½ pounds oxtail pieces

1 tablespoon avocado oil

2 tablespoons kosher salt

FOR THE BRAISE

1½ tablespoons olive oil

½ yellow onion, chopped

1 medium carrot, sliced

2 stalks celery, sliced

Kosher salt

2 tablespoons tomato paste

1. Preheat the oven to 425°F. Line a roasting pan with aluminum foil.

2. Using a paper towel, pat the oxtail pieces dry and place in the roasting pan. Drizzle on the avocado oil and use your hands to massage the oil into the meat. Season with the salt. Roast until the oxtails are nicely browned, about 40 minutes, flipping halfway through.

3. Once you've flipped your oxtails, start making the braising liquid: In a heavy pot or casserole such as a Dutch oven, heat the olive oil over medium heat. Add the onion, carrot, and celery, season with a pinch of salt, and cook until the vegetables are soft, 6 to 7 minutes.

recipe continues

Since I live alone, I often make this just for myself. I cook a couple of ounces of pasta while heating 1 cup of the oxtail ragu in a large pan. Once the pasta is cooked, I transfer it to the pan, along with a tablespoon of pasta water, mix it all together, and eat immediately, garnished with Parmesan cheese and parsley.

The meat sauce can be stored in the fridge for about 4 to 5 days. Towards the end, if I find myself unable to eat it all, I typically portion the sauce out into small airtight containers and freeze them for future use.

⅓ cup red wine, such as cabernet

One 14-ounce can crushed San Marzano tomatoes

1 whole head of garlic, cut in half crosswise

1 Parmesan rind (about 3x1 inches)

6 sprigs fresh thyme

2 bay leaves

½ teaspoon freshly ground black pepper

3 cups beef stock, plus more if needed

1 cup water

FINISHING TOUCHES FOR THE SAUCE

4 tablespoons cold unsalted butter, cut into pieces

1 teaspoon sherry vinegar

1 tablespoon sugar

10 ounces pappardelle pasta

Freshly grated Parmesan, for serving

Minced fresh parsley, for serving

4. Reduce the heat to medium-low and stir in the tomato paste. Cook, stirring, until the tomato paste darkens in color, about 4 minutes. Add the wine and, using a wooden spoon, stir well to deglaze, taking care to scrape up any browned bits from the bottom of the pot. Let the alcohol cook off for 1 minute, then add the crushed tomatoes and bring to a simmer.

5. By this point, your oxtails should almost be done. Transfer them to the pot; don't forget about the rendered fat that's inside the pan! Pour it into the pot as well (great flavor!).

6. Add the garlic, Parmesan rind, thyme, bay leaves, pepper, and beef stock. If the beef stock doesn't fully cover the oxtails, add more. Mix well and bring to a simmer. Partially cover the pot and simmer over low heat for 2 hours. Check on the braise periodically. Using a spoon, skim off any impurities that float to the top.

7. At the 2-hour mark, check on the braise: If the braising liquid has reduced and the oxtails are no longer fully submerged in the liquid, add 1 cup water (or enough to cover). Continue to cook for another 2 hours, until the oxtails are fork-tender. Discard the bay leaves, thyme, garlic, and Parmesan rind. Remove the oxtails and place them in a separate bowl. Let them cool before handling (about 15 minutes), then shred the meat with your hands and set aside.

8. Using an immersion blender or regular blender, blend the braising liquid until smooth. Bring back to a simmer over medium-low heat and reduce to a thicker sauce, about 10 minutes. Whisk in the butter, sherry vinegar, and sugar and continue to whisk until nicely emulsified. Taste and adjust seasonings. Remove from the heat and add the shredded oxtail to the mixture.

9. To serve, cook the pasta in a large pot of salted boiling water following the package instructions. In a large pan, heat the ragu over low heat. Once the pasta is done, use a spider strainer or tongs to transfer the pasta from the pot to the ragu pan (or combine the pasta and ragu in a large bowl if the pan isn't big enough). Add 5 tablespoons of the pasta water and mix well. Serve immediately, garnished with Parmesan cheese and parsley. Enjoy!

GINGER SCALLION LOBSTER

SERVES 2

FOR THE SAUCE

¼ cup chicken stock

2 tablespoons oyster sauce

1 tablespoon soy sauce

1 tablespoon sugar

2 teaspoons fish sauce

½ teaspoon freshly ground black pepper

FOR THE LOBSTER

Three 5-ounce lobster tails

1 tablespoon garlic powder

¾ cup cornstarch

Vegetable or canola oil, for frying

2 tablespoons avocado oil

5 scallions, cut in 1½-inch pieces, white and green parts separated

8 garlic cloves, minced

Two 1-inch pieces peeled fresh ginger, cut into thin matchsticks

2 serrano chiles, seeded and sliced

Drizzle of sesame oil

¼ teaspoon MSG

Freshly ground black pepper, for garnish

Chopped fresh cilantro, for garnish

Ginger scallion lobster is one of my favorite Chinese dishes. Growing up, I was only ever able to have it on certain special occasions, like weddings, birthdays, and at my rich cousin's house. When I say that my cousin was rich, I just mean that his family was the only one that didn't live in a mobile home. Now that I think about it, I actually don't even think he was my blood-related cousin.

Anyways, this dish is amazing in different ways. The lobster is battered and flash fried, allowing for the meat to be cooked thoroughly, but also remain really tender and sweet. It's then tossed in a sauce, along with the holy trinity of Chinese cuisine staples—ginger, scallion, and garlic. I opted for lobster tails to make this dish more affordable, without sacrificing any of the flavor. This is the perfect dish whenever I find frozen lobster tails on sale at the grocery store. Another reason I went for tails instead of whole lobsters is that not everyone is comfortable with slaying a whole live lobster, especially if you're new at cooking. This style of lobster is great served on top of Garlic Noodles (page 82).

1. For the sauce, mix all the sauce ingredients together and set aside.

2. For the lobster, cut each lobster tail in half lengthwise, then cut each half into three equal pieces to yield six pieces each, with the lobster meat still in the shell. Dry each piece of lobster with a paper towel and season with garlic powder. Place the cornstarch in a bowl, add the lobster pieces, and toss to lightly dust.

3. Fill a medium saucepan with 3 inches of oil and heat to 350°F over medium heat. Add half of the coated lobster pieces

recipe continues

and fry until golden, 1½ to 2½ minutes. Drain on a wire rack set inside a baking sheet or paper towel–lined plate. Repeat with the remaining lobster and set aside.

4. Heat the avocado oil in a wok or large pan over medium heat. Add the white parts of the scallions and the garlic and cook until fragrant, about 30 seconds. Add the sauce, fried lobster pieces, ginger, and serrano chiles. Mix well and cook for 45 seconds. Stir in the remaining scallion greens, the sesame oil, and MSG and cook for another 30 seconds to mix everything together. Remove from the heat.

5. To serve, transfer to a serving plate and top with black pepper and cilantro leaves. Enjoy!

When I first moved away from home, I was running on a high while exploring my new environment. I couldn't believe I was in a new city, in my first apartment, all by myself. I really felt like I was the main character in an indie movie. The feeling of being independent from your parents is so liberating. However, one of the biggest culture shocks was when it came to food. In Los Angeles, there are Vietnamese restaurants, but not many of them are good. As I explored L.A., looking for a Vietnamese restaurant that would satiate my cravings, I was disappointed time after time again. And that's when I realized that I took my hometown for granted. I missed the amazing Vietnamese food that San Jose provided, and most of all, I missed my mom's cooking.

When it comes to Vietnamese food, the majority of people think of phở, but there's many other dishes that are just as iconic. Try out other famous dishes like Bò Kho (Beef Stew), Thịt Kho Trứng (Caramelized Pork Belly with Eggs), and Bún Bò Huế (Beef Noodle Soup). Whether you're an outsider wanting to try cooking Vietnamese food for the first time, or a Vietnamese kid trying to re-create a meal to help with homesickness, these recipes won't disappoint.

7

MISSING HOME

MOM'S CHICKEN SALAD (GỎI GÀ)

SERVES ABOUT 6

When I moved away from home, I finally felt independent. However, I also felt like I had a hole in my heart because I missed my mom's cooking. My favorite salad in the entire world is Mom's chicken salad, her version of gỏi gà. It's actually funny because despite it being called a salad, it actually doesn't contain many vegetables other than Vietnamese coriander. Depending on the region in Vietnam, cabbage is incorporated, but that's it. This salad is every protein lover's dream. In my family, gỏi gà was served everywhere. Family parties, karaoke nights, birthdays, baby showers, funerals, graduation parties, death anniversaries—do we need more examples? Because I can keep going.

   We start with an entire chicken that is boiled and shredded, then seasoned and mixed with onions that are cut so paper thin that they might as well be translucent. But the star of it all? Vietnamese coriander. This special coriander has a certain smell that is so fragrant and addictive that it is capable of unlocking all of my childhood memories, and more. This is definitely a more-wholesome recipe, which I include because of how closely I hold gỏi gà to my heart. It's not the fanciest dish in the world, but to me it's the most important.

FOR THE POACHED CHICKEN

One 3- to 4-pound whole brown chicken (see Note), neck and head removed and discarded

1 yellow onion, peeled and halved

Two 1-inch pieces fresh ginger, sliced

2 tablespoons chicken bouillon powder (preferably Totole brand)

1. Place the chicken in a large pot and cover with water by 1 inch. Add the halved onion, ginger, and chicken bouillon. Bring to a boil over high heat. Reduce the heat to low and simmer until the internal chicken temperature reads 165°F all the way through, about 45 minutes.

2. Remove the chicken from the pot and place in a large mixing bowl/plate to cool down. The chicken will continue to cook.

3. Once the chicken is cool enough to handle (30 minutes or so), remove the meat from the bones and shred into bite-size pieces. Be sure to shred the chicken with the grain to create strands. Ripping against the grain will yield a mushy and unpleasant texture. (Traditionally, I use both the meat and chicken skin, but feel free to choose what you're comfortable with eating.) Place the meat in a large mixing bowl.

recipe continues

FOR THE SEASONINGS

Juice of 1½ lemons (about 3 tablespoons)

1½ tablespoons fish sauce

1 to 3 Thai chiles, sliced thin, to taste

1 tablespoon freshly cracked black pepper

1 teaspoon kosher salt

¼ teaspoon MSG

1 small yellow onion, sliced as thinly as possible

2 cups Vietnamese coriander leaves, torn in half

FOR SERVING

½ cup Fried Shallots (page 194)

Additional Vietnamese coriander

4. Season the chicken with the lemon juice, fish sauce, Thai chiles, pepper, salt, and MSG. Mix well. Add the sliced onion and mix well. Just before serving, mix in the Vietnamese coriander. Do not overmix. The order you mix in the ingredients is crucial. Make sure it's the seasonings, then the onion, and lastly the Vietnamese coriander. If you mix all the ingredients at the same time, the coriander will become soggy and lose its fragrant flavor.

5. Transfer to a serving plate and top with fried shallots and more Vietnamese coriander.

NOTE: *Brown chickens, readily available in most Asian grocery stores, are smaller, leaner, and tastier compared to other types of chicken. If you find it difficult to source in your area, feel free to substitute a small (3- to 4-pound) whole chicken.*

VIETNAMESE CORIANDER

Vietnamese coriander, or rau răm, is an herb widely used in southeast Asian countries. It's one of my favorite herbs to cook with due to its unique, addictive aroma, reminiscent of cilantro but spicier (it is sometimes called hot mint) and a bit lemony. The leaves are narrow and pointy, with burgundy markings. Use the young, tender leaves, as the older ones are tough and a bit bitter. You can find Vietnamese coriander in Asian markets.

GINGER CHICKEN (GÀ KHO GỪNG)

SERVES 2 TO 3

I love chicken. My favorite is fried chicken, but gà kho gừng is my second favorite—it also happens to be one of my mom's best dishes. I remember having this with a lot of julienned ginger, but as a kid I would try my best to avoid the ginger because if you accidentally bite into it, it'd ruin your whole meal. This dish is salty from the fish sauce, and just the right amount of sweet from the sugar. It's an easy one-pot recipe, making cleaning up and eating stress-free.

Typically, ginger chicken starts off with an entire chicken, butchered to pieces. My mom would use *all* parts of the chicken—yes, that means the head too. I remember having a friend over for dinner for the first time, and they let out a scream when they saw the chicken head in the pot. I won't traumatize you though. Today, we're going to be utilizing chicken wings, which are a lot less scary.

1½ tablespoons fish sauce

3½ tablespoons sugar

2 teaspoons garlic powder

1 teaspoon kosher salt

2 pounds chicken party wings (about 16 wings)

2 tablespoons avocado oil

4 garlic cloves, finely minced

1 shallot, finely minced

½ cup coconut soda (such as Coco Rico)

½ teaspoon freshly cracked black pepper

2 teaspoons fish sauce

Two 1-inch knobs fresh ginger, peeled and julienned

1 scallion, sliced

2 Thai chiles, sliced

A few sprigs fresh cilantro, torn into smaller pieces

1. Combine the fish sauce, 1½ tablespoons of the sugar, the garlic powder, and salt in a mixing bowl and mix well. Using a sharp knife, poke holes all over the chicken wings to allow the marinade to penetrate deeper. Add the wings to the bowl, toss well, and marinate in the fridge for at least 2 hours.

2. Heat the oil and remaining 2 tablespoons sugar together in a medium pan over medium-low heat. Stir periodically and cook until the sugar is an amber color, about 2 minutes. Add the garlic and shallot and cook, stirring frequently, until fragrant, about 45 seconds. Add the chicken and all of its marinade and mix well to get some color on the chicken. Then add the coconut soda. Bring to a simmer and cover with a lid. If you find that the liquid starts boiling, reduce the heat to low in order to maintain a simmer. Simmer, stirring every 10 minutes, for 30 minutes, until fully cooked through (internal temp should be at least 165°F).

3. Uncover, add the black pepper, fish sauce, and ginger, and mix well. Top with scallions, sliced chiles, and cilantro and serve with white rice. Enjoy!

STEAK AND EGGS (BÒ NÉ)

SERVES 1

FOR THE STEAK AND MARINADE

10 ounces boneless rib eye steak, cut into 1-inch cubes

1 tablespoon oyster sauce

1 tablespoon Maggi liquid seasoning

1 tablespoon avocado oil

1 teaspoon garlic powder

1 teaspoon sugar

½ teaspoon baking soda

FOR THE STIR-FRY

1 tablespoon avocado oil

½ yellow onion, sliced

10 cherry tomatoes

Pinch of salt

2 tablespoons unsalted butter

2 large eggs

FOR FINISHING

1 tablespoon Vietnamese cured pork liver pâté (optional)

Freshly cracked black pepper, to taste

1 scallion, sliced

A few sprigs fresh cilantro

Vietnamese baguette (bánh mì)

Vietnamese steak and eggs, or bò né, takes me back to the times my family visited Vietnam during summer breaks. In the mornings, we would eat at this insane breakfast restaurant that was suspended above water. You would literally take a wobbly rope bridge to access it, and underneath was a gigantic pond with a ton of koi fish. The first time I went to the restaurant, I refused to cross the bridge. In tears, I couldn't fathom the possibility of the bridge breaking, causing me to fall into the water and be eaten alive by fish. If only I had known that what was waiting for me across this bridge was one of the best Vietnamese breakfast dishes of all time.

The rough English translation of *bò né* is "dodging beef" because it's served on a sizzling-hot cast-iron plate and you literally find yourself dodging the splatters of butter and meat juices as it's being served. Good thing we're masters at dodgeball, am I right?

This Vietnamese sizzling plate contains juicy marinated steak, tomatoes, onions, and a runny egg that you eat with a freshly baked baguette. Oh yeah, it traditionally comes with a portion of pork pâté too, but I never really eat it because I'm a weenie, and don't like the thought of eating liver. One of my fondest memories of eating at this restaurant in Vietnam is being able to see all the koi fish swim peacefully in the pond. I would throw pieces of baguettes into the water and watch them swim after them.

recipe continues

1. Combine the steak and all the marinade ingredients in a bowl. Mix well, cover with plastic wrap, and marinate in the refrigerator for at least 30 minutes, or up to 2 hours.

2. Heat a heavy pan over high heat. Add the oil, along with the onion and cherry tomatoes, and season with a pinch of salt. Cook, stirring periodically, until the onion and tomatoes are slightly charred on the outside, 3 to 4 minutes. Remove from the pan and set aside on a plate.

3. Add the steak to the pan and cook over medium-high heat until nicely browned on the surface, about 4 minutes. Add the butter and give everything a quick toss. Transfer the beef to a plate.

4. Reduce the heat to medium-low and return the onion and tomatoes to the pan. (I like to keep the meat separate from the vegetables.) Crack the eggs into the pan and cook until the whites have set, 3 to 4 minutes. Set the steak on top of the onions.

5. If using, add the pork pâté, placing it in the middle of the pan. Top with freshly cracked black pepper, scallion, and cilantro. Serve from the pan, with a warm Vietnamese baguette.

PHỞ

SERVES 6

The most universally known Vietnamese dish is phở. There are many different variations—chicken, seafood, vegetarian—but the phở I like the most is classic beef phở. It's a dish that I can't live without. My mom would make it for me whenever I was sick, and add extra white onions and sriracha. She said that would help me get better faster. Did it? Maybe, but what I know is that I was sweating because it was so spicy.

Eventually, I went from eating phở when I was sick from a cold or flu to eating it whenever I was hungover after a night of drinking. I feel like it cures all headaches and dehydration, and it overall brings me back to life. If it's cold or rainy outside, eat phở. I will warn you though, this phở is definitely one of the more time-consuming recipes in this book. It requires a *lot* of prep work and calls for simmering the broth for almost 6 hours. Unless you're cooking for a family or group of friends, I would just order from your favorite local phở restaurant. But if you're trying to impress your family or a Vietnamese boo's family, make phở.

4 pounds beef bones

2½ pounds short ribs (about 6 pieces)

3 yellow onions, sliced in half end to end, skin left on

3 large shallots, sliced in half end to end, skin left on

1 medium knob fresh ginger, sliced in half

FOR THE AROMATICS

6 star anise

2 cinnamon sticks

4 black cardamom pods

1 tablespoon coriander seeds

1 tablespoon fennel seeds

5 cloves

1. Combine the beef bones and short ribs in a large stockpot. Cover with warm water and bring to a boil over high heat. Boil for 5 minutes, then drain. Rinse with cold water to get rid of any debris, then return to the empty stockpot. Set aside.

2. Pace a wire grill rack over your burner and set to medium-high heat. Roast the onions, shallots, and ginger directly over the flame, turning often, until they are charred and slightly softened. If you are using an electric or induction stove you can roast the items directly on the burners. Onions will take about 5 minutes, and shallots/ginger will take around 3 minutes. Set aside to cool until you can handle them, then peel and discard the charred skins. Remove any burnt parts, and transfer to the stockpot.

3. For the aromatics: Heat a dry small pan over medium heat, add all the aromatics, and toast until slightly toasted on the outside and fragrant, about 3 minutes. Transfer to a spice bag or a square of cheesecloth, and tie the bag with cooking twine. Add to the stockpot.

recipe continues

FOR THE BROTH

About 4 quarts warm water

1 tablespoon kosher salt

6 tablespoons fish sauce

3½ ounces (100g) rock candy

1 tablespoon Vietnamese chicken bouillon powder (preferably Totole brand)

FOR ASSEMBLY AND GARNISH

12 ounces Vietnamese meatballs (bò viên), available in Asian groceries (see sidebar)

2 pounds rice noodles (banh pho), cooked according to package instructions

½ bunch fresh cilantro, chopped

1 yellow onion, thinly sliced

4 scallions, sliced

SUGGESTED SIDES AND SAUCES

8 ounces bean sprouts

1 bunch fresh Thai basil

1 jalapeño chile, sliced

2 limes, sliced

Sriracha

Hoisin sauce

4. Fill the stockpot with enough warm water to cover the beef bones and short ribs, about 4 quarts. Bring to a boil, cover partially, and reduce the heat to maintain a gentle simmer. Simmer for 3 hours.

5. Remove the aromatics bag, onions, shallots, and ginger and discard. Transfer the short ribs to a plate and let cool to room temperature, then refrigerate. Meanwhile, cover the pot and let it simmer for 3 more hours.

6. About 15 minutes before the finished cooking time, season the broth with the salt, fish sauce, rock candy, and chicken bouillon.

7. To assemble: Add the meatballs to the broth. Heat the short ribs up in the microwave until warmed through, about 1 minute.

8. Each bowl gets some noodles, followed by one short rib. Divide the meatballs evenly among the bowls, then ladle on the hot broth, to taste. Top with cilantro, onions, and scallions. If you like, serve with your choice of bean sprouts, Thai basil, sliced jalapeño, lime slices, sriracha, and hoisin.

VIETNAMESE MEATBALLS (BÒ VIÊN)

Vietnamese meatballs come in different varieties, some pork, some beef, others a combination. They can contain cartilage or not. You'll find them in the meat aisle in Asian groceries, usually packed in vacuum-sealed packets.

VIETNAMESE BEEF STEW (BÒ KHO)

SERVES 4 TO 5

Bò kho is the perfect dish to showcase our history with the French. The French colonized Vietnam in the late 1800s until 1954, and during that time we picked up a lot of French culinary ingredients and techniques that contributed to some of our most popular dishes. Bò kho is the Vietnamese version of the French beef bourguignon, made with stewed beef, potatoes, and carrots. This yummy stew is always paired with a crusty Vietnamese baguette, which we also adopted from the French. One of my favorite things about bò kho is that you have to use your hands to eat it: Tear off a piece of baguette and dip it in the stew for a few seconds for the bread to soak up the juices. D E L I S H !

If you don't finish it today, you can have it the next day and the day after that—the flavors don't change really. As time passes, the flavors actually seep into the potatoes and carrots, making it more and more delicious. Although people eat bo kho with noodles or rice, I like it the classic way. Baguette, please!

FOR THE BEEF AND MARINADE

1½ pounds chuck roast, cut into 1½-inch cubes

1 tablespoon brown sugar

1 tablespoon fish sauce

1 teaspoon Chinese five-spice powder

½ teaspoon freshly ground black pepper

½ teaspoon kosher salt

FOR THE STEW

3 tablespoons avocado oil

½ large shallot, minced

3 garlic cloves, minced

4 tablespoons tomato paste

One 12-ounce can coconut soda (preferably Coco Rico)

1. Combine the chuck and all of the marinade ingredients in a mixing bowl and mix well. Cover and marinate in the fridge for at least 1 hour, or up to 24 hours.

2. Heat a Dutch oven or other heavy pot over medium-high heat. Add 2 tablespoons of the avocado oil and half of the marinated chuck steak. Brown on all sides, 2 to 3 minutes; set aside on a large plate. Repeat with the remaining chuck steak.

3. Reduce the heat to medium. Add the remaining 1 tablespoon avocado oil, along with the shallot and garlic, and cook until fragrant, about 45 seconds. Add the tomato paste and cook until slightly browned, 2 to 3 minutes. Return the browned meat, along with any meat juices on the plate, to the pot and add the coconut soda and water. Mix well and bring the mixture to a boil, then reduce the heat to a low simmer. Add the star anise, ginger, cinnamon stick, and lemongrass. Using a skimmer, skim any foam that may arise at the top and discard. Partially cover and simmer for 2 hours.

recipe continues

2½ cups water

2 whole star anise

2 slices fresh ginger, about ¼ inch thick

1 cinnamon stick

3 lemongrass stalks, bottom 5 inches of tender parts only, bruised

2 carrots, peeled and cut into 1-inch pieces

2 Yukon Gold potatoes, peeled and cut into 1-inch cubes

2 tablespoons fish sauce

2 tablespoons brown sugar

¼ teaspoon MSG (optional)

Freshly ground black pepper, to taste

Fresh cilantro, for garnish

4 to 5 Vietnamese baguettes, toasted

4. Add the carrots and potatoes. Cover and continue cooking until the carrots and potatoes are tender, about 45 minutes.

5. Remove the star anise, ginger, cinnamon stick, and lemongrass stalks and discard. Season the stew with the fish sauce, brown sugar, and MSG (if using), and give it a stir before removing from the heat.

6. Ladle into serving bowls and top with pepper and cilantro. Accompany with a toasted Vietnamese or French baguette, and enjoy!

NOTE: *If not eating right away, allow the braise to cool to room temperature before covering and transferring to the fridge. When ready to eat, transfer to microwave-safe bowls and heat up in the microwave in 1-minute increments until warmed throughout. This stew lasts up to 3 days in the fridge.*

FREE GAME

Browning the ingredients (meat, tomato paste, etc.) is a crucial step in this recipe because it creates immense depth of flavor!

VIETNAMESE SPICY BEEF NOODLE SOUP (BÚN BÒ HUẾ)

SERVES ABOUT 8

FOR THE BROTH

3 pounds pork neck bones

2 pounds beef bones

2 pounds raw pork hocks

2½ pounds beef shanks

2 yellow onions, peeled and halved

3 shallots, peeled and halved

2 slices fresh ginger (about ¼ inch thick)

12 stalks lemongrass, cleaned, bruised, and cut in half

1 tablespoon kosher salt

6 quarts (24 cups) water

FOR THE BÚN BÒ HUẾ SPICY OIL (AKA SATE OIL)

¼ cup vegetable or canola oil

1 tablespoon annatto seeds

3 garlic cloves, minced

1 shallot, minced

1 tablespoon minced lemongrass

2 tablespoons gochugaru (Korean pepper flakes)

Ahhh, the famous dish of my people. Huế people. Our dialect is deep and strong just like our spicy bún bò huế—filled with flavors of beef, shrimp paste, and aromatic lemongrass. My mom would make this all the time, no matter if it was hot or cold outside. The soup, even just the smell, brings back so many memories of visiting Vietnam. In the summer heat, we would sit outside on plastic chairs and scarf down bowls of bún bò huế until we couldn't breathe anymore.

This is the only recipe in this book that contains Vietnamese shrimp paste, because that shit is no joke. The smell of shrimp paste is strong enough to send someone into a coma. Rest assured, the taste is a lot better than the smell. If you've never cooked with it before, you're in for a damn treat.

1. For the broth: Place the pork bones, beef bones, and pork hocks in a large stockpot, cover with warm water, and bring to a boil over high heat. Boil for 5 minutes. Drain and run the meat and bones under cold water. Using your hand, scrub away any debris that is left on the bones.

2. Rinse the pot and discard any debris that may be stuck to the sides. Return it to the stove and return all of the rinsed meat and bones, along with the beef shank, halved onions and shallots, ginger, lemongrass, and salt. Add the water and bring to a boil. Reduce to a simmer. Using a skimmer, skim off any scum that may rise to the top. Partially cover with a lid and simmer for 2 hours.

recipe continues

FOR THE SEASONINGS

3 to 5 Thai chiles (depending on spice level), sliced

½ cup fish sauce

1¾ ounces (50g) rock sugar

2 tablespoons chicken bouillon powder (preferably Totole brand)

1½ tablespoons Vietnamese shrimp paste (preferably Lee Kum Kee brand)

½ teaspoon MSG

Kosher salt, to taste

FOR ASSEMBLY

2 pounds rice vermicelli noodles, cooked following package instructions

10 ounces Vietnamese sausage (chả lụa), cut into slices, then half circles

½ yellow onion, thinly sliced

¼ bunch fresh cilantro, chopped

¼ cup chopped Vietnamese coriander

3 scallions, sliced

FOR THE FRESH HERB PLATE

¼ red cabbage, thinly shredded

¼ green cabbage, thinly shredded

½ bunch Vietnamese coriander

½ bunch fresh mint

1 jalapeño chile, sliced

8 lime wedges

3. Remove the pork hocks. If you don't eat pork hocks, feel free to discard them at this point. Or let them cool to room temperature, then refrigerate until serving. (I don't enjoy pork hock, so I toss them at this point. Traditionally, they're reheated and added back to the soup for serving, as below.) Remove and discard the shallots, onions, and ginger. Partially cover the pot and continue simmering for another 2 hours.

4. Remove the beef shanks, let cool to room temperature, then cut into thin slices. Keep the broth simmering, with the lid off, while you make the spicy oil.

5. For the spicy oil: Heat the oil in a small pan over medium heat. Add the annatto seeds and cook until the oil turns red, about 1 minute. Strain the oil and return to the pan. Add the garlic, shallot, lemongrass, and gochugaru and cook until fragrant, about 2 minutes. Scrape the contents of the pan into the simmering broth.

6. To season the broth, add the chiles, fish sauce, rock sugar, chicken bouillon, shrimp paste, MSG, and salt to taste. Stir together until the shrimp paste and rock sugar fully dissolve.

7. To assemble each serving of bún bò huế: Place cooked noodles in each bowl, followed by a few slices of beef shank and sausage. If using, warm up your pork hocks in the microwave for 1 minute, and add to the bowls. Ladle broth from deep inside the pot over it all, then add a ladle of some of the spicy oil from the top.

8. Garnish with thinly sliced onion, cilantro, Vietnamese coriander, and scallions. Serve hot, passing the fresh herb plate at the table.

NOTES: *Pork necks, pork hocks, and beef bones are available at all Asian grocery stores in the butcher section, meat section, or frozen meat section.*

Vietnamese shrimp paste is available at most Asian grocery stores in the jarred sauce aisle.

Vietnamese pork sausage is available at Vietnamese delis that sell Vietnamese sandwiches (bánh mì), or in the frozen section at Vietnamese grocery stores. These are more difficult than the rest to obtain. If you can't find them, feel free to omit from the recipe.

CARAMELIZED PORK BELLY WITH EGGS (THỊT KHO TRỨNG)

SERVES 4

Thịt kho trứng is responsible for traumatizing an entire generation of Vietnamese American kids. Whenever my mom made it, I understood that this was the only thing that we would be eating for the next week. However, moving away from home means that you can grow to miss it. I'm tired of eating these organic and gluten-free meals in L.A. Give me something that reminds me of home.

Thịt kho trứng literal translation is "meat braised with egg," which is why you can choose from a variety of meat cuts to create the dish. In my opinion, pork belly is too fatty and can be tiresome to eat. So I typically use pork shoulder, which is leaner and healthier—but you can use other cuts, like pork rib, as well. This is Vietnamese cooking, don't be too shy to get flexible with it! Whenever I make this dish for myself, I continue the tradition of finishing it over the course of a few days. Luckily, thịt kho trứng actually becomes more flavorful as the days go by, since the braising liquid has more time to penetrate the meat and eggs. Let's trauma bond <3.

FOR THE MEAT AND MARINADE

1½ pounds pork belly or pork shoulder, cut into bite-size (about ¾-inch) cubes, or pre-cut pork ribs (1 to 2 inches in length)

1 shallot, minced

1 tablespoon fish sauce

1 teaspoon freshly ground black pepper

½ teaspoon kosher salt

1. Combine the pork and all of the marinade ingredients in a mixing bowl. Mix together well and marinate at room temperature for 30 minutes.

2. For the braise: Heat a medium pot over medium heat. Add the oil and sugar and stir occasionally with a heatproof rubber spatula to prevent the sugar from burning. Cook until the caramel is an amber color, 2 to 3 minutes. Stir in the pork and all of its marinade and cook until the pork is lightly browned on all sides, about 5 minutes total. Add the water, coconut soda, and garlic and bring to a boil over medium heat. Reduce the heat to maintain a simmer. Using a skimmer, skim any impurities that may float to the top and discard. Cover partially with a lid and braise for 1 hour.

recipe continues

1 tablespoon vegetable or canola oil

3 tablespoons sugar, plus more for serving

1½ cups water

One 12-ounce can coconut soda (such as Coco Rico)

4 garlic cloves, peeled and slightly smashed

8 large eggs

1½ tablespoons fish sauce, plus more for serving

¾ teaspoon kosher salt

3 Thai chiles, thinly sliced on the diagonal

3. While the pork is braising, hard boil the eggs: Fill a medium pot with 2 inches of water and bring to a boil over medium-high heat. Carefully add the eggs and boil for 8 minutes. Meanwhile, fill a mixing bowl with water and ice. Transfer the eggs to the ice bath and leave until cool enough to handle, about 5 minutes. Peel the eggs and set aside.

4. After 1 hour, uncover and season the pork braise with the fish sauce and salt. Add the hard-boiled eggs and Thai chiles. Do not cover, and continue cooking, stirring occasionally, until the braising liquid has reduced slightly and the eggs are warmed through, about 15 minutes.

5. Season to taste with additional fish sauce, sugar, and salt if desired. Remove from the heat and serve with white rice.

TURMERIC FISH WITH DILL

SERVES 2 TO 3

FOR THE MARINADE

1 tablespoon avocado oil

1 tablespoon chopped fresh dill

1½ teaspoons fish sauce

1½ teaspoons chicken bouillon powder (preferably Totole brand)

2 teaspoons sugar

1½ teaspoons turmeric powder

1 teaspoon garlic powder

¼ teaspoon kosher salt, plus an additional pinch

FOR THE FISH

1 pound catfish fillets

2 tablespoons vegetable or canola oil

1 small yellow onion, sliced

Kosher salt

4 garlic cloves, minced

2 scallions, cut into 2-inch segments

1 bunch fresh dill, chopped

Crushed peanuts (optional)

To me, dill has got to be one of the most pleasant culinary smells. Dill on turmeric fish though? Chef's kiss.

Turmeric fish was introduced to me at a restaurant called Thien Long when I was in elementary school. I watched as the server brought out this giant sizzling plate of yellow, slightly charred fish that had this addictive aromatic smell. I would sit there, playing Pokémon Green on my Game Boy Advance as my mom fed me all night.

Be careful not to wear clothes that you like when you're making this recipe, because turmeric is *strong* and will stain anything that it touches yellow. If you get it on your clothes, it's game over. This is why I typically cook this naked.

1. In a small bowl, mix all ingredients for the marinade and set aside.

2. Cut the catfish fillets into 2-inch pieces. If the fillets are thick, cut them in half horizontally into thinner slices. Transfer to a large ziplock bag. Add the marinade, seal, and move the bag around between your fingers to mix the fish and the marinade together well. Transfer to the fridge and marinate for at least 2 hours, or up to 12 hours.

3. Heat a 10-inch skillet over medium heat and add 1 tablespoon of the oil. Once the oil is hot, add the fish, and cook until nicely browned, about 2½ minutes. Flip the fish onto the other side and continue cooking until an internal temperature of 145°F, 2 to 3 minutes. Transfer to a plate.

4. Heat the remaining 1 tablespoon oil in the pan and add the onion and a pinch of salt. Cook for 1 minute. Add the garlic and scallions, mix well, and continue cooking for 30 to 45 seconds, until aromatic. Remove from the heat.

5. Lay the pieces of fish over the ingredients in the pan, top generously with fresh dill and optional crushed peanuts, and serve.

CARAMELIZED FISH (CÁ KHO TỘ)

SERVES 2

"Cá kho tộ with rice smacks. It's my favorite Vietnamese dish," says my sister, Yvonne. Okay, and . . . ? Girl, ain't nobody asked you. It's true though, there's nothing quite like eating a bowl of cá kho tộ with white rice. I'm literally drooling just thinking about it.

I remember as a kid, my family and I used to eat dinner on the floor. Our dining table was a couple sheets of newspaper, and on top of that would be a spread of proteins, veggies, and soup. If I saw cá kho, it would be my lucky day. I think it's a common thing to take your mom's cooking for granted. But then, once you move over 500 miles away, you won't be able to eat your favorite foods anymore. This is especially true for me because a lot of Vietnamese food in DTLA is mid (at best). Finding myself in a desperate situation, I had to call my mom to give me a step-by-step live demonstration on how to make the incredible caramelized fish that she used to feed us. The most important part of this dish is getting the caramelization right. When cooking sugar, there's about a 20-second room for error between it being the right color and burnt/bitter. As soon as the sugar turns a nice brown color, it's go time! The actual cooking is a piece of cake.

FOR THE FISH AND MARINADE

1 pound catfish fillets, cut into 2- to 3-inch pieces

2 tablespoons kosher salt

3 garlic cloves, minced

2 small shallots, minced

1 tablespoon fish sauce

1 tablespoon sugar

FOR THE SAUCE

½ cup coconut soda (preferably Coco Rico)

¼ cup water

1 tablespoon fish sauce

1½ teaspoons sriracha

1. To clean the catfish, place in a large mixing bowl, add the salt, and rub it into the fish for 30 seconds. Rinse the fish with cold water and pat dry with a paper towel. Dry the bowl and return the fish to the bowl.

2. Add the remaining marinade ingredients to the bowl, mix well, cover, and transfer to the fridge to marinate for at least 30 minutes, or up to 1 hour.

3. Combine all the sauce ingredients in a small bowl, mix well, and set aside.

4. When ready to cook, heat the oil and sugar together in a medium clay pot or medium frying pan over medium-low heat. Cook, stirring the sugar occasionally, until the sugar caramelizes to a nice brown color, 4 to 6 minutes. The time for caramelizing sugar can vary because we all have different types of burners, varying in strengths. Pay close attention to

recipe continues

FOR COOKING AND FINISHING

1 tablespoon avocado oil

2 tablespoons sugar

3 Thai chiles, cut into slices using scissors

½ teaspoon freshly cracked black pepper

1 Fresno chile, sliced

1 scallion, sliced

the color! Once the sugar is a nice brown color, feel free to move on to the next step of the recipe.

5. Add the fish, pretty sides facing down, and all of the marinade to the caramel in the pot and cook for 4 minutes. Add the sauce and flip the fish pieces over. Bring to a simmer over medium-low heat, cover partially with a lid, and cook for 20 minutes. If the heat is too high, reduce to maintain a simmer.

6. Remove the lid, add the Thai chiles, and cook uncovered for another 15 minutes, until the cooking liquid has reduced. Add the black pepper, Fresno chiles, and scallion, and serve with rice. Enjoy!

GRILLED MUSSELS WITH SCALLION OIL (CHEM CHÉP NƯỚNG MÕ HÀNH)

SERVES 2 TO 3

1 pound frozen half-shell mussels (see Note)

2 scallions, thinly sliced

3 tablespoons vegetable or canola oil

⅛ teaspoon kosher salt

4 tablespoons salted butter, melted

½ teaspoon freshly ground black pepper

2 tablespoons Fried Shallots (page 194)

1½ tablespoons crushed roasted peanuts

Lemon wedges, for serving

Chopped fresh cilantro, for serving

Tabasco, for serving

During my time working at a Vietnamese restaurant, it was common for me to be exhausted during my shift. When you work at an Asian restaurant, you're not really designated to any specific role, but are expected to do a bit of everything. I wish I would've told my bosses, "Do I look like Clark Kent to you?" A lot of the time, the pay *never* matches the amount of work we do. But I digress.

Reflecting on my time as a server, I think what I miss most is the relationships I had with the nighttime kitchen staff. We all knew that we didn't want to be there, but had to—whether it was for money, or the fact that we weren't college educated and felt this was the only job we could find.

Knowing this, we would take care of each other whenever we could. I would bring the kitchen staff water and soda during their shifts. In some cases when they had hard days, I'd sneak them a couple beers to get turnt. During shifts when I was tired from handling 10+ tables by myself, they would make me these mussels without me asking. That's what I call love.

I could clear two dozen of these mussels at a time. Each bite is so satisfying because the shell serves as a delivery vehicle to bring the mussels straight into your mouth. At first, you're met with the crunchy fried shallots and bits of crushed peanuts—texture. Then comes a plethora of scallion in a pool of salted butter. Then lastly, you bite into the plump mussel.

This mussel dish is impossible to mess up even for the most beginner cook. That's because the mussels are already cooked through when bought. All we're doing is heating them up to be warm throughout and adding our finishing touches for flavor and texture. Just be careful of overcooking them, as mussels tend to turn really chewy.

recipe continues

1. To defrost the mussels, place in a large mixing bowl and cover with cold water. Allow to defrost for 15 minutes, replacing the water halfway through.

2. While the mussels are defrosting, make the green scallion oil: Place the sliced scallions in a heatproof cup, such as a Pyrex measuring cup. Heat the vegetable oil to 350°F in a small saucepan over medium heat. This should take 1 to 2 minutes. Pour the hot oil onto the scallions. Season with salt, mix well, and set aside.

3. Drain the mussels. Release the mussels from their shells by running a butter knife underneath each mussel. Using paper towels, dry the insides of the shells as well as the mussels and return the mussels to their shells. (It's important to dry mussels well to prevent the end product from being soggy.) Place the mussels on a wire rack set in a baking sheet.

4. Preheat the broiler to 450°F. Spoon butter evenly onto each individual mussel. Season each mussel with a pinch of black pepper, and spoon on the green scallion oil. Place in the top part of the oven and broil until the butter starts bubbling and the mussels are warm all the way through, 3 to 4 minutes.

5. Remove from the oven and top each mussel with fried shallots and crushed peanuts. Serve with lemon wedges, cilantro, and Tabasco.

NOTE: *You can find frozen half-shell mussels in Asian markets.*

Dessert? I've heard of that before . . . *lights up a cigarette*. Back in the day, I used to be crazy about desserts. It's true. I even have ten cavities to prove it. I indulged in everything sweet. Chocolate, Butterfingers, lollipops, sour belts, Lucas candies, ice cream, Coca-Cola—you name it. My parents used to ask me, "Wow, that's so sweet. How can you possibly eat so much of that?" Pfft. They don't know what they're talking about. They're just hating because they're old heads.

I became an old head. My desire for super sweet desserts disappeared like the Last Avatar. I don't know where it went. Nowadays, when I eat things that are sweet, I have to worry about it showing in my gut. I hate it here. I still crave sweets from time to time, though. Which is why in this chapter, I'm going to share with you some of my favorites to cook up. My absolute favorite from this list is tiramisu. I love coffee so much, and tiramisu is just a gift from above. Especially if you pair it with a slightly bitter coffee.

8

ROOM FOR DESSERT

APPLE CRUMBLE WITH ICE CREAM

SERVES 2

1 teaspoon unsalted butter, for the ramekins

FOR THE APPLE FILLING

1½ Granny Smith apples, peeled, cored, and cut into approximately ½-inch dice (about 2 cups)

¼ cup packed brown sugar

1 tablespoon lemon juice

1½ tablespoons cornstarch

½ teaspoon ground cinnamon

Pinch of kosher salt

FOR THE CRUMBLE TOPPING

⅓ cup rolled oats

¼ cup packed brown sugar

¼ cup all-purpose flour

½ teaspoon ground cinnamon

4 tablespoons unsalted butter, melted

FOR SERVING

2 scoops vanilla ice cream, or ice cream of choice

Caramel syrup, to taste

Special equipment: two 6-ounce ramekins

In high school, I had a good friend named Hoan. He and I were little, scrawny boys when we met, and we shared a common interest—the gym. He was my gym buddy, my fitness bro, but also my biggest enabler because he would always convince me to eat with him at Denny's.

After school, we would walk half a mile to the gym, lift weights, and then end up at the Denny's in the same plaza as our gym. There we would order a sizzling fajita plate and share an apple crisp with ice cream that would essentially wipe out all the gains we'd been working hard for in the previous two hours. Not only does this dessert pack on a ton of calories, but it pairs cold ice cream with warm apple crumble—a combination that's sure to mess up your enamel. What was his way of justifying it? "Don't worry! We're just dirty bulking. Just wait until we cut weight, we're gonna look ripped."

Well, eight years later, it seems like I'm still dirty bulking. Don't worry though, my diet starts Monday (I totally didn't say that last week). Hoan had a lot more discipline than I did though, because he ended up becoming a personal trainer and competing in bodybuilding shows, and I became a food influencer. This recipe is my version of the dessert that I shared with one of my good childhood friends. Hoan, if you're reading this, F you.

recipe continues

1. Preheat the oven to 350°F and position a rack in the middle. Butter two 6-ounce ramekins with ½ teaspoon soft butter each. It's easiest to use your finger to rub the butter all over the inside of the ramekin. Set aside.

2. For the filling, combine the diced apples, brown sugar, lemon juice, cornstarch, cinnamon, and salt in a mixing bowl and toss together well. Divide equally between the two prepared ramekins.

3. For the topping, in a medium mixing bowl, combine the oats, brown sugar, flour, and cinnamon and mix well. Add the melted butter and mix until the mixture resembles a crumble that holds its shape. It should somewhat resemble wet sand. Divide equally between the two ramekins.

4. Place the ramekins on a small baking sheet. Bake until the apples are soft all the way through and the crumble is nicely browned, 38 to 40 minutes.

5. Allow the apple crumble to cool for 3 to 4 minutes. Top each one with a scoop of ice cream, followed by a generous drizzle of caramel syrup, and serve. Enjoy!

CHEESECAKE WITH STRAWBERRY COMPOTE

MAKES ONE 9-INCH CAKE, SERVING 12

Throughout my cooking journey, I've made my mom *hundreds* of meals. I've used some of the best and most expensive ingredients and researched for hours to re-create different meals from a variety of cultures. But there's only one thing that has left an impression in her mind—my cheesecake. I'm not joking when I say my cheesecake makes her emotional. This one time she bought a cheesecake from Costco and cried while eating it because she said it wasn't good enough. She called me on the phone to tell me how much she missed when I lived at home because I would make her the best cheesecake. Okay, buddy. When she decided to finally visit her son in Los Angeles, I decided to bake and surprise her with an entire cake, and she was jumping for joy. She loved it so much that she even froze the extra cake in Tupperware containers to take home with her to San Jose. What a weird woman.

What sets my cheesecake apart from others is that it's not too sweet. That's the ultimate Asian compliment when it comes to desserts. Also, it's not as heavy as other cheesecakes. You can eat it and still continue about your day! When baking this delicate dessert, make sure to turn off the oven at the right time, and allow it to cool down gradually. You want to stop the baking when the cheesecake still has a jiggle in the center (the inner 30 percent) and is firm around the edges. In this recipe, we really take our time with the cheesecake by letting it cool with the oven door slightly open, then transferring it to room temp. This is to ensure that the cake's surface layer doesn't crack from temperature shock. The cake will naturally firm up completely overnight in the fridge.

FOR THE CRUST

10 sheets graham crackers

¼ cup sugar

⅛ teaspoon kosher salt

7 tablespoons unsalted butter, melted, plus 1 tablespoon for brushing pan

1. Preheat the oven to 350°F and position the oven rack in the bottom third.

2. For the crust: Break up the graham crackers into the bowl of a food processor fitted with the steel blade. Process to a powder, about 1 minute. Add the sugar and salt and pulse until fully blended. Transfer to a medium mixing bowl and add 7 tablespoons of the melted butter. Using a spatula, mix well.

3. Using a pastry brush, brush the remaining butter on the inside of a 9-inch springform pan. Add the crust mixture. Use the bottom of a measuring cup or spatula to even out the

recipe continues

FOR THE FILLING

Four 8-ounce packages cream cheese, at room temperature

1 cup sugar

1 cup sour cream, at room temperature

2 teaspoons lemon juice

1½ teaspoons pure vanilla extract

3 large eggs, at room temperature

Boiling water

Strawberry Compote (recipe follows), for topping

crumbs and press down into the bottom of the pan. Bake until the crust has slightly darkened in color, about 15 minutes.

4. Use a spatula to press down on the crust once more. Allow the crust to cool for 10 minutes, then wrap the bottom of the pan with two sheets of aluminum foil. This will prevent water from seeping into the pan during baking. Reduce the oven temperature to 325°F.

5. For the filling: In a large mixing bowl, use a hand mixer to cream together the cream cheese and sugar until very smooth, about 2 minutes. Add the sour cream, lemon juice, and vanilla. Using a spatula, mix once more until thoroughly combined. Add the eggs and mix until barely combined.

6. Strain the filling through a fine-mesh sieve into the springform pan, using a spatula to push the filling through the sieve. Lift the pan up and slam it a couple times on your kitchen counter, to allow any air bubbles to rise to the top. Using a spatula, level out the batter until even. Place the cake pan in a larger pan or baking dish (I use my 12-inch cast-iron skillet).

7. Transfer the pans to the oven, and carefully fill the outer pan with enough boiling water to come halfway up the sides of the cheesecake pan. Bake until the middle of the cheesecake is still slightly jiggly, about 55 minutes. After the 40-minute mark, keep an eye on your cake! Depending on the oven, your cheesecake may start to brown. If so, cover the top with a sheet of aluminum foil.

8. Turn off the oven and open the oven door slightly. Allow for the cake to cool in the oven for 30 minutes.

9. Remove from the oven, remove the pan from the water bath, and allow to cool fully to room temperature (about 1 hour). Wrap with plastic wrap and refrigerate for at least 4 hours, or overnight.

10. If you see any condensation on top of your cheesecake, gently lay on a paper towel to absorb the moisture. When ready to serve, release the springform pan's side, and cut the cake into 12 even slices with a sharp knife. Top with strawberry compote. Enjoy!

To make a smooth cheesecake, it's important to cream the cream cheese and sugar together until it's *really* smooth. But as you're mixing in the eggs, avoid overmixing, as this will create too much air in the batter. This is the reason we use the hand mixer *only* to cream the cream cheese and sugar, and mix everything else with a spatula.

STRAWBERRY COMPOTE

MAKES ⅔ CUP

6 large strawberries, hulled
2 tablespoons sugar
1 tablespoon lemon juice

1. Cut the strawberries into ½-inch cubes and combine with the sugar and lemon in a medium pot. Place over medium heat, stir together, and bring to a boil. Reduce the heat to low and simmer, stirring occasionally, until the compote reduces enough to coat the back of a spoon, 13 to 14 minutes.

2. Let cool for 2 to 3 minutes before using as a topping for the cheesecake.

CINNAMON ROLLS

MAKES 9 ROLLS

FOR THE DOUGH

1 cup whole milk

4 tablespoons unsalted butter

1 large egg

2 tablespoons granulated sugar

1 teaspoon salt

One ¼-ounce packet instant yeast

3½ cups all-purpose flour, plus more as needed

Oil, for oiling the mixing bowl

FOR THE FILLING

7 tablespoons unsalted butter, softened, plus 1 tablespoon for buttering the pan

½ cup lightly packed dark brown sugar

1 tablespoon ground cinnamon

¼ cup heavy cream

FOR THE ICING

4 ounces cream cheese, softened

4 tablespoons unsalted butter, melted

2 tablespoons whole milk

2 teaspoons lemon juice

1 cup confectioners' sugar

Cinnamon rolls will always remind me of the times when my friends and I hung out at the Eastridge mall. Having nothing to do, we would walk around, trying to see what kind of debauchery we could get into. One fond memory is being intoxicated by the smell of the cinnamon rolls, wafting in the air as the employees of Cinnabon worked their magic. There's nothing quite like it.

In the front, they had this small tray containing free cinnamon roll samples, and my friends and I would compete with each other on how many free samples we were capable of "stealing." Each of us would take turns walking by, and grab handfuls of samples at a time. It got to the point where the employees got annoying and stopped handing samples as a whole. Ughhh, buzzkill. Am I right? They act like the samples are coming out of their paycheck. *rolls eyes*

Anyways, we're beyond those days of abusing free samples. Cinnamon rolls are my favorite things to bake at home. Especially in the cold winter months, baking cinnamon rolls is such a wholesome activity to do with your friends—not to mention it makes the house smell amazing. Every time I take a bite into this warm, gooey dessert that is dripping in icing, I'm reminded of my childhood again.

The recipe makes plenty of icing, for those who prefer to spread it extra thick!

recipe continues

1. For the dough, combine the milk and butter in a small saucepan and warm over medium-low heat, just until the butter is fully melted. Remove from the heat and allow to cool to lukewarm.

2. Combine the egg and granulated sugar in the bowl of a stand mixer and whisk together well. Slowly add the milk and butter mixture. Add the salt and yeast and continue to whisk until well combined.

3. Place the bowl on the mixer fitted with a dough hook. Set the speed to medium, and slowly incorporate the flour. If any flour sticks to the side of the bowl, quickly scrape with a spatula. Continue kneading for 5 minutes. Humidity affects the consistency of the dough. You may need to use a little more flour if your kitchen is humid. The dough should be bouncy and slightly sticky. If you find that the dough is too wet, add more flour, no more than 1 tablespoon at a time, until it reaches the desired consistency, just a little tacky. It should not be dry.

4. Brush a mixing bowl with oil and place the dough in it. Cover with plastic wrap. Set in a warm, draft-free spot (like an empty oven) and leave to proof until the dough has doubled in size, about 1 hour 15 minutes. The amount of time that it takes for the dough to rise depends on the humidity and temperature. The more humid and warm the environment, the faster the dough will rise.

5. While the dough is rising, clean the surface you will use for rolling out your dough, and prepare the filling: Mix together the 7 tablespoons softened butter, brown sugar, and cinnamon. Generously butter an 8x8-inch baking pan with the remaining tablespoon of butter.

6. When the dough has doubled in size, remove the plastic wrap and punch down the dough to deflate. Lightly dust your work surface with flour and place the dough on top. Using a rolling pin, roll out the dough to a 13x19-inch rectangle, about ¼ inch thick. Using a small spatula, spread the cinnamon sugar filling evenly over the dough, leaving a ¾-inch border along the edges.

7. Place the rectangle with a long edge closest to you and, beginning from that bottom edge, roll up the dough into a tight cylinder. Pinch a seam along the finished edge to ensure

the roll is sealed and won't break apart. Using a floss string or sharp knife, cut 1½ inches from both ends, and then slice the roll into nine equal pieces (you can discard the ends or bake them separately as a little snack). Place the rolls in the buttered 8x8-inch baking pan with their prettiest side facing up. Cover with plastic wrap. Allow the rolls to proof a second time, until they fill the baking pan, 40 to 45 minutes.

8. Preheat the oven to 350°F and position a baking rack in the middle. Spoon the cream evenly over the rolls. Bake until the tops are slightly brown, 25 to 30 minutes.

9. While the rolls are baking, make the icing: In a medium mixing bowl, combine the cream cheese, butter, milk, and lemon juice. Whisk until smooth. Gradually whisk in the confectioners' sugar until smooth. Set aside. (I have come to realize that some people prefer a thick icing, while others prefer a looser icing. To adjust the icing to your liking, you can add more milk or confectioners' sugar. The milk will thin out the icing and the sugar will make it thicker.)

10. Let the rolls cool for 2 to 3 minutes. Using a rubber or offset spatula or a spoon, spread the icing all over the cinnamon rolls. Serve immediately while the rolls are hot! Cover leftovers with plastic wrap and refrigerate for up to 3 days. When ready to eat, you can pop them in the microwave for a minute for a quick bite.

VIETNAMESE COFFEE TIRAMISU

SERVES 9

Tiramisu is every coffee addict's dream dessert. It's an Italian dessert that consists of layers of coffee-soaked ladyfingers and mascarpone cheese cream, with a dusting of cocoa powder on top. Tiramisu has such a delicious flavor profile with the bitterness of the coffee balancing the sweetness of the creamy cheese filling. I opted to take a more personal approach by dipping my ladyfingers in Vietnamese coffee, instead of the traditional espresso.

Vietnamese coffee is personal to me, because I've seen my parents make it every morning since I was a kid. It's traditionally brewed in a phin (a Vietnamese coffee filter) that sits on top of a cup, and you watch it do its magic as the coffee slowly drips down. It's a lot stronger and slightly more bitter than regular espresso!

One of my favorite things to pair with tiramisu is a plain iced Americano. This is the only time I'll ever drink coffee without milk in it (black coffee by itself is absolutely vile and all the actors in Korean dramas are lying to you).

4 large egg yolks

½ cup sugar

Two 8-ounce packages mascarpone, at room temperature

1 cup heavy cream

2 teaspoons pure vanilla extract

1 cup brewed Vietnamese coffee (like Café Du Monde), or any strong coffee, at room temperature

2 tablespoons coffee liqueur, preferably Kahlúa (leave out if you don't drink alcohol)

32 ladyfingers (about one and a half 7-ounce packets; see Free Game, page 176)

1 to 2 tablespoons cocoa powder

1. Bring ½ cup water to a boil in a small saucepan. Meanwhile, combine the egg yolks and sugar in a large heatproof mixing bowl. Once the water starts boiling, place the mixing bowl on top of the saucepan, making sure the bottom of the bowl is not touching the water. Vigorously whisk the eggs and sugar together, until the color of the yolks is light yellow, about 1 minute. Remove from the heat. Add the mascarpone cheese to the eggs and sugar and mix well until smooth.

2. Combine the cream and vanilla in another large mixing bowl. Using a hand mixer, beat the cream until it forms soft peaks. (Soft peaks are when you lift your whisk and the cream in the bowl comes up and drops down; imagine a Santa hat.) Be careful to not overmix, because we don't want our cream to turn to butter. If this happens, add a couple tablespoons of heavy cream and gently beat to fix.

3. Using a spatula, fold the egg mixture into the cream mixture until barely combined. Note: fold, don't mix! We want to keep all the air in the cream that we worked hard to get. Set aside.

recipe continues

4. In a soup plate, mix the coffee with the Kahlúa. Take the ladyfingers and quickly dip them on all sides, then use to line the bottom of an 8x8-inch square cake pan. (Don't soak the ladyfingers too much! Quickly dip them. Soaking will end up making the tiramisu soggy and unpleasant to eat.) Repeat until you've covered the bottom of the pan with ladyfingers. If needed, use a knife to cut them so that they fit.

5. Pour half of the cream mixture on top of the lady fingers. Using a spatula, level the cream out so it is evenly spread throughout the pan. Be sure to push the cream down into the corner and side areas, to make sure there aren't any air bubbles, so you don't end up with a loose tiramisu.

6. Repeat with the remaining ladyfingers and cream. Using your spatula, smooth out the top of the cream.

7. Wrap the pan with plastic wrap and transfer to the fridge. Allow the tiramisu to set overnight, or for at least 12 hours.

8. When ready to eat, remove from the fridge. Cut into nine equal pieces and dust with cocoa powder. Transfer to a serving plate, and enjoy!

FREE GAME

Depending on the size of your ladyfingers, you may use less (or more) for each layer than the recipe calls for. Any leftover ladyfingers can be wrapped and used when you make this again! :)

CRÈME BRÛLÉE

SERVES 3

Crème brûlée is every beginner's introduction to an "upscale" dessert. It's easy to make and introduces technical baking skills that can be applied to other recipes. You know, things like steeping vanilla beans, creaming yolks and sugar, and using a water bath and blowtorch. To me, crème brûlée was one of those iconic desserts that I've always seen in American movies and restaurants, and I didn't fully get the hype until I tried it myself. Translated as "burnt cream" from French, it has this slightly burnt, hard sugar topping that you break into with your spoon. The body of the desert is a rich, smooth, creamy custard that slowly melts in your mouth. It's definitely a great dessert for those who are feeling indulgent, or want to celebrate a special occasion, like a romantic anniversary? Who am I kidding, if you're reading this you're definitely single. But feel free to make this for yourself for your birthday!

1 vanilla bean

2 cups heavy cream

5 large egg yolks

⅓ cup sugar

Pinch of salt

FOR TOPPING

2 tablespoons sugar

Fresh berries, like blueberries, raspberries, blackberries (optional)

6 mint leaves

Special equipment: Kitchen torch and three 6-ounce ramekins

1. Preheat the oven to 300°F and position a rack in the lower third.

2. Using a small knife, split the vanilla bean in half and scrape the seeds into a small saucepan. Add the pod and the cream. Place over medium heat and heat just to a simmer, about 5 minutes. Do not allow it to boil. Turn off the heat and let the vanilla pod and seeds steep in the cream for 5 minutes.

3. Meanwhile, in a mixing bowl, combine the egg yolks, sugar, and salt. Whisk until lightened in color, about 1 minute. Set aside.

4. Once the vanilla is done steeping, remove the pod from the cream. To temper the egg yolk mixture with the hot cream, whisk in just a few tablespoons cream at a time into the yolk mixture until all of the cream has been added and is fully incorporated.

5. Set up another mixing bowl with a strainer. Pour the custard through the strainer into the bowl. (Straining ensures a smooth crème brûlée.) Remove the foam from the top of the custard by gently grazing the surface with a paper towel.

recipe continues

The foam should stick to the paper towel. If there's excess foam, skim with a spoon. (It's important to skim the foam to ensure that we have the smoothest-looking crème brûlée!) Divide the custard equally among three 6-ounce ramekins and place the ramekins in a 9x13-inch baking dish. Lift and slam the ramekins a couple times to bring any air bubbles to the surface.

6. Fill the baking dish with enough boiling water to come halfway up the ramekins, then carefully transfer to the oven. Bake until the outer edges of the crème brûlées are set, but the middles still have some jiggle, 35 to 40 minutes.

7. Remove the baking dish from the oven. Remove the ramekins from the water bath and set aside on the counter to cool for 1 hour. When cool enough to touch, cover with plastic wrap and transfer to the fridge for at least 4 hours, or for up to 3 days.

8. When ready to serve, uncover the ramekins. Using a paper towel, blot any moisture that may have accumulated on the surface. Top each crème brûlée with 2 teaspoons sugar, spread evenly over the top. Using a blowtorch, torch the sugar on the top until it's nice and caramelized throughout. If you don't have a blowtorch, you can use your oven's broiler to caramelize the sugar. Let rest for at least 1 minute to allow the sugar to set.

9. Top with fresh fruits of choice if desired, and one or two mint leaves. Enjoy!

CHURROS WITH CHOCOLATE GANACHE

MAKES 16 TO 18 MINI CHURROS

FOR THE CHURROS

1 cup water

6 tablespoons unsalted butter

2 tablespoons sugar

½ teaspoon ground cinnamon

½ teaspoon pure vanilla extract

Pinch of kosher salt

1 cup all-purpose flour

3 large eggs

Vegetable or canola oil, for frying

FOR THE CINNAMON SUGAR

½ cup sugar

1 teaspoon ground cinnamon

Chocolate Ganache (recipe follows), for serving

Special equipment: Piping bag with a closed star tip (Ateco #846), which you can get online or at specialty cooking stores

Growing up as an immigrant in San Jose means being dragged by your parents to the San Jose Flea Market on the weekends. My mom was at the flea market more often than any of the employees ever were. She might as well have gotten a job there and worked her way up to be the CEO of the place.

But I hated it. Since I was young, the idea of walking amongst big crowds for long periods of time exhausted me. And what was even more exhausting was holding bags of clothes for my mom as she haggled with the vendors for deals on more clothes for the family.

My mom knew I hated it, but she knew I could be bribed to tag along for the low price of a churro. There was no shame in my game. The fresh smell of fried dough mixed with cinnamon sugar is warm enough to put a smile on any kid's face—especially mine.

Churros are one of the more straightforward dessert "snacks" to make. Unlike the rest of the desserts in this book, we're going to be deep-frying, making them a lot faster to make. The hardest part is making sure you have the right star tip in your piping bag. Star tips vary in shapes and sizes, which will affect your cooking times and the appearance of your churros. In this recipe, I'll be using the Ateco #846 pastry tip.

recipe continues

1. Combine the water, butter, sugar, cinnamon, vanilla, and salt in a medium pot and bring to a simmer over medium heat until the butter melts. Add the flour all at once and stir vigorously with a rubber spatula over medium heat until the flour is fully incorporated and no lumps remain. Remove from the heat and allow the mixture to cool for 10 minutes.

2. Mix in one egg at a time until thoroughly combined. At first, it might look like it won't mix together, but you just need to keep going at it. Mix until smooth. Transfer the churro dough to a piping bag with a closed star tip (Ateco #846).

3. In a medium pot, heat about 2 inches of oil to 350°F. Carefully pipe in 5 to 6 inches of the churro dough, then cut it off with scissors. Repeat until you have four churros frying at once. Fry the churros for 2 to 3 minutes on each side, turning them until they're golden brown all over. You can gauge your frying time by first testing one churro to see how it turns out! Remove each finished batch from the oil and drain on a paper towel–lined tray.

4. Repeat batches to fry about 18 churros. (Make sure your oil is at a constant temperature of 350°F. When you add the churros to fry, the temperature of the oil will naturally drop a bit. Bring it back to 350°F between batches.)

5. Mix together the cinnamon sugar and place in a wide shallow bowl. Once the churros are fully drained, lightly coat with cinnamon sugar by giving them a quick toss in the bowl. Don't toss freshly fried churros with sugar without draining first, as the oil droplets will make the sugar clump up.

6. Serve with the chocolate ganache.

FREE GAME

If your churros are nicely browned on the outside but a bit undercooked in the middle, the oil might be too hot. Try lowering the temperature and cooking for a longer time period.

If your churros turn out too hard, you might be cooking them for too long and the oil temperature may be too low. Turn up the heat slightly and try again!

CHOCOLATE GANACHE

3½ ounces dark chocolate bar
3½ ounces heavy cream
¼ teaspoon flaky salt

1. Using a knife, cut the chocolate bar into ½- to ¼-inch pieces and transfer to a heatproof bowl.

2. Bring the cream to a simmer in a small saucepan. Pour over the chocolate, then wait 15 seconds before stirring the two together.

3. Add the salt, and continue stirring until the chocolate is fully melted. If the cream cools too much before all of the chocolate has melted, microwave in 10-second increments and stir in between.

Every superhero movie has a protagonist. You know, the main character that goes through trial and error, learns life lessons, someone close to him dies, and then he goes and fights supervillains? They're loved by everyone in the city and are constantly in the spotlight. However, they don't accomplish their goals alone. They're often accompanied by supporting acts who make such huge differences, but are often overlooked. Justice for supports! They need love too. </3 This is a chapter about all the small "mini" recipes that I think play a great role in leveling up our main dishes.

9

JUSTICE FOR THE SUPPORT

CAJUN BUTTER

MAKES ½ CUP

If you think regular butter is good—*ouuuwee*! Just wait until you try this. I first discovered Cajun butter when I was getting dinner with friends at a restaurant called Gem. As a free appetizer, restaurants normally serve bread with salted butter. However, Gem was different because they gave us Cajun butter. Spicy, garlicky, with a hint of sweetness—this butter had my friends and me wanting *more*. We even asked for a second serving. LOL.

My favorite use for this butter is to melt it with a blowtorch over a nice rib eye steak (like on page 123). If you're planning to serve it with bread, cut off some slices of butter and allow them to soften at room temperature before serving.

½ cup (1 stick) unsalted butter, softened

8 cloves Garlic Confit (page 191)

2 teaspoons smoked paprika

1 teaspoon cayenne pepper

1 teaspoon minced fresh thyme

½ teaspoon onion powder

½ teaspoon sugar

¼ teaspoon kosher flaky salt

¼ teaspoon lemon juice

1. Combine all of the ingredients in a mixing bowl and mix well with a fork until thoroughly combined.

2. Lay out plastic wrap on your work surface and transfer the butter mixture onto the wrap. Roll the butter into a log shape, wrap in the plastic, then refrigerate until ready to serve, at least 1 hour.

3. Wrapped tightly, the butter keeps in the refrigerator for up to a week.

PICO DE GALLO

MAKES ABOUT 1 CUP

Pico de gallo is a tasty Mexican salsa that will have your taste buds singing like a mariachi band. Although great year-round, my favorite time of the year to make pico is in late spring/ early summer since that's the best time for tomatoes in California. Since it doesn't require many ingredients, their quality plays a big factor on taste. Enjoy this salsa on Carne Asada Crispy Tacos (page 69), or with a side of tortilla chips as a snack!

2 Roma tomatoes, cored, seeded, and diced

⅓ medium white onion, diced

1 jalapeño chile, stemmed and minced

¼ cup minced fresh cilantro

Juice of 1 lime

¼ teaspoon kosher salt, plus more to taste

1. Combine the tomatoes, onion, jalapeño, and cilantro in a bowl. Mix well. Season with the lime juice and salt. Taste for salt and add more if needed.

2. Cover and refrigerate for at least 30 minutes, or up to 3 days to allow the ingredients to marinate and slightly pickle.

3. When ready to eat, serve alongside tacos or tortilla chips and enjoy!

Orange Salsa,
page 190

Guacamole,
page 5

Pico de Gallo,
page 187

ORANGE SALSA (VERY SPICY)

MAKES ABOUT 1 CUP

One of San Jose's cultural monuments is La Vic's, a long-standing taqueria, known for serving good Mexican eats. It was especially popular amongst the younger crowd as it naturally became the unofficial meeting spot after a night of drinking. I have a vague memory of my friends and I, completely plastered, with our bodies on 1 percent battery, stuffing our faces with the carne asada fries with extra orange sauce.

It became a popular thing amongst restaurant goers to eat at the restaurant and steal the bottle of their delicious salsa. It got to the point where the restaurant realized they had no choice but to bottle it up and sell it. Give the people what they want. I had to include my variation of this orange salsa so all of you can get a taste of what eating at La Vic's is like. This sauce is a variation of salsa roja, where tomatoes, garlic, onions, and chiles get blistered and blended with oil, chicken bouillon, and water. The result? A smoky, garlicky sauce that is fucking *spicy*. I like to serve it with Carne Asada Tacos (page 69) and Fish Tacos (page 74).

¼ cup plus 2 tablespoons olive oil

3 Roma tomatoes, quartered, cored, and seeded

1 small yellow onion, peeled and quartered

6 garlic cloves, peeled

½ teaspoon kosher salt, or more to taste

½ cup dried chiles de arbol, seeded if you want less spice

2 tablespoons water

Juice of ½ lime

½ chicken bouillon cube (I prefer Knorr)

1. Heat ¼ cup of the olive oil in a skillet or pan over medium heat and add the tomatoes, onion, garlic, and salt. Cook for 5 minutes, stirring constantly, until the tomatoes are starting to soften. Add the chiles de arbol and continue to cook for another 5 minutes, stirring constantly, until the chiles, onion, and garlic are browned.

2. Transfer everything to a blender and add the remaining 2 tablespoons olive oil, the water, lime juice, and chicken bouillon. Blend on medium speed until smooth, about 1 minute. (If you find that the salsa isn't becoming smooth, let the ingredients sit in the blender for 5 minutes to soften the chiles before blending on high again.)

3. Taste the salsa and adjust for salt. I typically add ¼ teaspoon at this point, but feel free to add more to your taste.

4. Serve with tacos or any dish you'd want to flavor with additional spice. If you don't plan on using it immediately, transfer to an airtight container and store in the fridge for up to 7 days.

GARLIC CONFIT

MAKES ABOUT 30 CLOVES

If there's one thing that I am, I am a garlic guy. Have you ever tried eating raw garlic? Of course not, because it has way too much of a strong bite and is too bitter. The only people I know who eat raw garlic are older Asian people. That's because they're built differently. Once you've survived a war in your home country and fled to America, nothing scares you anymore.

Garlic confit is truly elite. By confiting, you take away garlic's bite and actually make it somewhat sweet—more palatable for those with weenie taste buds like you and me. One of the reasons I love it so much, besides its heavenly flavor, is that it's so versatile. We use garlic confit throughout this book—in Cheesy Garlic Bread (page 8) and Hummus (page 2). Sometimes I just eat it spread on toast.

If you're a fellow garlic lover and have the time, I highly recommend giving garlic confit a try—just be prepared to have your breath smell like garlic for the next week. If you don't have the time (something that we're all running low on nowadays), screw garlic confit. Stick to regular minced garlic or garlic powder. I don't blame you.

3 heads garlic (about 30 cloves)

2 tablespoons avocado oil

1 teaspoon kosher salt

1. Preheat the oven to 375°F and position a rack in the middle.

2. Cut off the top part of each garlic head, about one-fourth of the way down from the tip. Cut two squares of aluminum foil, large enough to envelop the three heads of garlic. Stack the two squares and place the garlic in the middle, cut sides up. Drizzle the avocado oil onto the top of the garlic heads to cover and season with salt. Wrap the garlic heads in the aluminum foil, making sure they are completely sealed.

3. Place the foil packet on a small baking sheet and bake until the garlic is nicely roasted and soft throughout, about 1 hour. Let the garlic cool until you can handle it, about 5 minutes.

4. There's two ways to go about removing the garlic confit from its skin. The more visually satisfying way is to squeeze

recipe continues

it out, like toothpaste. However, some of the garlic will be squashed and trapped inside the skin. The way to extract the most garlic is to use a fork to pierce the skin, then scoop out the roasted garlic.

5. If not used immediately, place the confit in an airtight jar and cover with more oil. Refrigerate as soon as possible. It lasts in the refrigerator for up to 2 weeks. But when stored improperly, garlic confit can produce a serious toxin that causes botulism, a fatal illness. Be careful to keep track of how long your garlic confit has been in the fridge, and don't go over! Foodborne illnesses are no joke.

NOTES: *You don't always have to use 30 cloves of garlic. You can adjust the amount depending on how much you need. Make as little as 1 clove or up to 100. Just make sure to adjust your oil so that the garlic is completely submerged.*

In recipes that use garlic confit, I like to assume that 1 head of garlic yields about 10 cloves of garlic confit.

FRIED GARLIC

MAKES ¼ CUP FRIED GARLIC AND 2 TO 3 TABLESPOONS GARLIC OIL

Garlic is good in every form, whether you include it in stir-fries, confit it into a paste, or dehydrate it into a powder to sprinkle on everything. Fried garlic is used as a finishing topping in a lot of Asian cuisines. You can buy it premade at Asian grocery stores, but I (along with all the aunties) love to make it myself. All you have to do is mince up a bunch of garlic (or pulse it in the food processor) and fry in oil until lightly golden brown. Throughout this book, we'll use it to make Garlic Green Beans (page 33) and Fish Sauce Wings (page 42). But feel free to adventure and add it to anything that you think needs a garlicky, crispy boost.

¼ cup vegetable or canola oil
12 garlic cloves, minced
Pinch of MSG

1. Place a strainer over a heatproof bowl and set aside.

2. Heat the oil in a medium saucepan over low heat. Once hot, add the minced garlic and cook, stirring constantly with a spatula to ensure that it cooks evenly, until it's a light blond color, 2 to 3 minutes. (Pay close attention to the garlic's color because it will continue to cook once it's strained. If you strain too late, it'll cook into a burnt and bitter mess.)

3. Drain the garlic through the strainer, catching the oil in the bowl. Then transfer the garlic to a paper towel–lined plate, spreading it out to prevent clumping. Allow to cool to room temperature, about 5 minutes. Once cooled, season with MSG and mix well.

4. Seal the crispy garlic in a container with a lid and store at room temperature for up to a week.

5. The by-product of making fried garlic is garlic oil! Once cooled, store it in an airtight container in the fridge for up to a month. The oil is flavorful, and can be used to replace any oil when cooking savory foods for an extra layer of flavor.

FRIED SHALLOTS

MAKES ½ CUP FRIED SHALLOTS AND ABOUT ½ CUP SHALLOT OIL

Have you ever had or made a dish that was missing something? Yeah, it's the fried shallots. It's commonly used in Vietnamese dishes as the final garnish that adds another layer of flavor and crunchy texture. Shallots are part of the onion family, the one that makes you cry when cutting them.

Unlike fried garlic, we don't mince these. We start by thinly slicing them from head to root. This is where you want to bust out your sharpest knife, or mandoline. We fry them until slightly golden and season with a touch of MSG. It's very easy and fun to make, and they add depth of flavor + umami to any dish you choose. In this book we use fried shallots to make my Mom's Chicken Salad (page 134), Grilled Mussels with Scallion Oil (page 159), and Cantonese Steamed Fish (page 90).

¾ cup vegetable or canola oil

1 cup sliced shallots (about 3 shallots)

Pinch of MSG

1. Place a strainer over a heatproof bowl and set aside.

2. Heat the oil in a small saucepan over low heat. Add the shallots and fry gently, stirring occasionally, until a light golden color, 6 to 7 minutes. (It's important to take the shallots out when they are a light golden color, as they will get darker as they cool. We want to avoid burning the shallots, as that will make for a really bitter taste. It's okay if not *all* of the shallots are golden.)

3. Drain the shallots through the strainer, catching the oil in the bowl. Transfer the shallots to a paper towel–lined plate to drain off excess oil. Let the shallots cool down for 5 minutes. Once cooled, transfer to a container, season with MSG, and mix well.

4. Store the fried shallots in an airtight container at room temperature for up to a week.

5. The by-product of making fried shallots is shallot oil! Once cooled, store it in an airtight container in the fridge for up to 1 month. The oil is flavorful and can be used to replace any oil when cooking savory foods, for an extra layer of flavor.

Caramelized Onions, page 196

Garlic Confit, page 191

Fried Garlic, page 193

Fried Shallots, page 194

CARAMELIZED ONIONS

MAKES ½ CUP

Cooking can sometimes be hectic. Like when you're making a stir-fry, you need to be fast or you'll burn something. Other times, it's as simple as stirring things around every couple minutes while watching a show on your phone. When making caramelized onions, we'll be channeling our inner monk and practicing patience. Because as time-consuming and boring as cooking caramelized onions is, the results are so worth it. And trust me, I would never make you spend so much time cooking a vegetable if I thought it tasted like cheeks.

Caramelized onions are my secret weapon when it comes to recipes like Smash Burgers (page 76), because the unique sweetness takes burgers to another level.

2 medium yellow onions (see Note)

1 tablespoon avocado oil

½ teaspoon sugar

¼ teaspoon kosher salt

1. Cut the onions in half lengthwise and peel back the first layer. Cut off the stem and root ends, and slice thinly from stem to root. (The direction you cut the onion is important. We cut from stem to root so the onion retains its structure when cooking. If you cut crosswise, the onion breaks down under heat.) Set aside.

2. Heat a nonstick pan or pot over medium heat. Add the onions, along with 1 cup water. Cover with a lid and allow the onions to soften until the water has evaporated, about 15 minutes.

3. Drizzle the oil over the onions. Using a spatula, mix the onions to evenly coat them in oil. Continue cooking, uncovered, until you see brown bits develop on the edges of the onions. Then stir in ½ tablespoon water to prevent the onions from burning. Using a rubber spatula, give the onions a stir and then spread them out over the pan. Repeat, adding water and spreading out the onions occasionally, until the onions are an amber brown color, 12 to 14 minutes. It's important to not stir too often, as it'll interfere with the caramelization process. Try stirring every 5 or so minutes, lowering the heat if you find your onions are coloring too quickly.

NEWT

4. Once the onions are adequately caramelized, continue cooking to get rid of any excess liquid. Season with the sugar and salt and give the onions one last mix. Remove from heat and use immediately.

5. If not used immediately, allow the onions to cool to room temperature before storing in an airtight jar in the refrigerator for up to 1 week.

NOTE: *The quantity of onions might seem like a lot at first, but they'll shrink by 90 percent by the time you're done with them. So, if you're looking to make a lot of caramelized onions, remember to scale appropriately!*

UNIVERSAL CONVERSION CHART

OVEN TEMPERATURE EQUIVALENTS

250°F = 120°C

275°F = 135°C

300°F = 150°C

325°F = 160°C

350°F = 180°C

375°F = 190°C

400°F = 200°C

425°F = 220°C

450°F = 230°C

475°F = 240°C

500°F = 260°C

MEASUREMENT EQUIVALENTS

Measurements should always be level unless directed otherwise.

⅛ teaspoon = 0.5 mL

¼ teaspoon = 1 mL

½ teaspoon = 2 mL

1 teaspoon = 5 mL

1 tablespoon = 3 teaspoons = ½ fluid ounce = 15 mL

2 tablespoons = ⅛ cup = 1 fluid ounce = 30 mL

4 tablespoons = ¼ cup = 2 fluid ounces = 60 mL

5⅓ tablespoons = ⅓ cup = 3 fluid ounces = 80 mL

8 tablespoons = ½ cup = 4 fluid ounces = 120 mL

10⅔ tablespoons = ⅔ cup = 5 fluid ounces = 160 mL

12 tablespoons = ¾ cup = 6 fluid ounces = 180 mL

16 tablespoons = 1 cup = 8 fluid ounces = 240 mL

INDEX

Note: Page references in *italics* indicate photographs.

INDEX

HarperCollins books may be purchased for educational, business, or sales promotional use. For information, please email the Special Markets Department at SPsales@harpercollins.com.

FIRST EDITION

DESIGNED BY RENATA DE OLIVEIRA

Photographer: Andrea D'Agosto
Photo Assistant: Ashli Buts
Food Stylist: Nathan Carrabba
Food Stylist Assistants: Courtney Weis and Diana Kim
Prop Stylist: Jaclyn Kershek
Photo Studio: Historic Hudson Studios

Library of Congress Cataloging-in-Publication Data has been applied for.

ISBN 978-0-06-330477-2

24 25 26 27 28 IMG 10 9 8 7 6 5 4 3 2 1